Devotional Insights for Moms

From the Mouths of BABES

Conover Swofford

BARBOUR
PUBLISHING

Print ISBN 978-1-61626-541-0

eBook Editions:
Adobe Digital Edition (.epub) 978-1-62029-000-2
Kindle and MobiPocket Edition (.prc) 978-1-62029-001-9

Published by Barbour Publishing, Inc., P.O. Box 719, Uhrichsville, Ohio 44683
www.barbourbooks.com

Our mission is to publish and distribute inspirational products offering exceptional value and biblical encouragement to the masses.

Member of the
Evangelical Christian
Publishers Association

Printed in the United States of America.

CONTENTS

INTRODUCTION

The Bible says that children, the greatest gift God has entrusted to us, are a heritage from the Lord. They are the future of our families, our churches, and our world. We are to love, pray for, discipline, and enjoy our children. We are also to teach them the Word of God when at home, when walking along the road, when we lie down, and when we rise up (see Deuteronomy 11:18–19). Knowing our children will walk in truth is something we can celebrate joyously (see 2 John 4). How wonderful that God created each one of our children individually and placed them with us, their parents, selectively. To make this an awesome match, parents are to recognize that they are blessed to have children and endeavor to be a blessing to them in return.

Psalm 127:4–5 describes children as arrows in the hand of a warrior, and happy is the person who has a quiver full. At times, mothers may think their quiver is a little too full and its arrows a little too sharp because children can hit a myriad of targets, coming up with unique observations, astounding assumptions, and scathingly truthful comments, often with side-splitting results. There is no denying that our children are often a hilarious heritage.

This devotional came about after many years of listening to children say the most amazing things. The following 180 stories—based on comments that came directly "out of the mouth of babes" (Psalm 8:2; Matthew 21:16 NKJV)—are full of wisdom and truth from a child's perspective. They are funny and yet quite practical on many levels. We have children asking for chicken pox, wondering how to spell *TV*, and much more.

But in Jesus' day, children weren't thought of too highly. Yet He used them as illustrations to teach His disciples astounding truths. For example, when His disciples wanted to know who would be the greatest in the kingdom, Jesus told them they needed to become like a child to even *enter* the kingdom (see Matthew 18:3). His meaning? God wants us to trust in and rely on Him, just like our children fully trust in and rely on us. Children are sincere in their beliefs, sensitive to the moods of others, and have simplicity in their outlook. It is only with the simplicity, trust, and dependence of a child that we enter God's Kingdom.

Through our children, God gives us new perspectives on spiritual truths, and He also gives us practical applications of those truths. If we listen, we can let the things our children say teach us more about our Father God.

Let us embark on this journey with our children as we listen to what they have to teach us. Hopefully this devotional will be a blessing to all who read it.

BEING THANKFUL

"FOUR AND A NICKEL"

"I prayed for this child.
The Lord has given me what I asked him for.
So now I'm giving him to the Lord.
As long as he lives he'll be given to the Lord."
1 SAMUEL 1:27–28 NIrV

Two four-year-old boys were having a conversation.
The first one said, "I'm four and a quarter."
The second one replied, "Then I'm four and a nickel."

When Hannah prayed and asked God for a son, she promised the Lord that she would give her child back to Him. Sometime later, God answered her prayer and Hannah gave birth to Samuel. As soon as the boy was weaned, she took him to the temple to serve God, visiting Samuel only once a year. Hannah understood that children are gifts to us, on loan to us from God. Today, we recognize Hannah's wisdom by dedicating our own children to the Lord and by teaching them about God and how to live their lives for Him. This is our way not only of thanking God, but of giving our children back to Him, even though we may not physically part from them as Hannah did Samuel. Our children may not understand what a blessing they are until they have children of their own. In the meantime, we can teach them to be grateful for God's love, strength, and forgiveness. Having children is an awesome responsibility, a tremendous blessing, and an occasion to daily give thanks to God. Because of them, we can rejoice, just like Hannah.

No matter how young or old we are, we can be thankful to God.

God's Angles

*The Law of the LORD is perfect; it gives us new life.
His teachings last forever, and they give wisdom to ordinary people.*
PSALM 19:7 CEV

*A six-year-old boy came home from Sunday school
and proudly told his mother,
"Today we learned about God and His angles."*

Many people in this world seem to think that you have to have some kind of angle to get ahead. Fortunately for us, God doesn't have any angles. He's not always looking out for Number One even though He is the ultimate Number One. Instead, God looks out for us. He gave us His perfect law and His perfect Son. The verse above says that God's law revives our souls, the seat of our emotions. When we are depressed or disappointed or hurting, we can read God's Word to be revived and refreshed. How wonderful to have the psalms to uplift and inspire us when we need it most. When Paul and Silas were beaten and thrown into jail, they were singing, most likely some of the psalms, at midnight. In the midst of pain and imprisonment, they were praising God and thanking Him. (See Acts 16:16–40). The result? Their prison doors opened and their chains were loosed! We can learn from the example of Paul and Silas. Whatever happens, we can see God's hand in it and know that it is for our good.

We are thankful that God has angels, not angles.

10

Everlasting God

Before the mountains were brought forth or ever
You had formed and given birth to the earth and the world,
even from everlasting to everlasting You are God.
PSALM 90:2 AMP

A grandmother was sitting on the sofa when her seven-year-old
granddaughter came in. With a thoughtful look on her face,
the child stood staring at her grandmother.
"What is it?" the grandmother asked.
"Are you older than God?" her granddaughter asked.
Smiling, the grandmother said, "No, God is much older than I am."
"Well, then," the girl said, "are you older than Jesus?"

Age is a relative thing. To a ten-year-old, twenty seems ancient. To anyone over forty, a twenty- year-old seems like a baby. Just like our children have trouble comprehending how old we are, so we have trouble comprehending how long God has been around. *Everlasting* is a concept that boggles our minds. God always has been, is, and always will be. Because we live in time, we think everything should have a beginning. Yet God has no beginning. He has no end. Our finite minds cannot comprehend this mystery. But we don't have to understand it to be thankful for it. As everlasting as God is, so is His everlasting love for us. His love for us has no beginning and it has no end. What an amazing truth. Thanks be to God!

God is love, so His love is as everlasting as He is.

Never Too Old

*The older women likewise, that they be reverent in behavior,
not slanderers, not given to much wine, teachers of good things.*
TITUS 2:3 NKJV

*When a five-year-old girl came home
from her first day at kindergarten,
her grandmother asked her, "Did you like your teacher?"
"She was old," the girl replied. "Real old. Not as old as you, but old."*

We are never too old to serve our God. He has things for us to do all throughout our lives here on earth. As we get older and more mature in our Christian walk, God specifically wants us to be "teachers of good things." In Titus 2, Paul says that the older women are to teach the younger women to be good wives and mothers and keepers of their homes. Being a keeper of the home doesn't mean housekeeping. It means making sure that your family's home life is secure in the Lord. God entrusted women with this duty because man is the head of the family and woman is the heart. All our lives we can influence others. We can be good examples. We can pass on our knowledge and wisdom. We can always help someone with something. A housebound ninety-five-year-old woman spent her days praying for her family and writing encouraging letters. At her funeral, her family members stood and read the letters she had written to them. Her influence over them did not stop with her passing.

**Thank God that, no matter how old we are,
He has something for us to do in His service.**

Saying Grace

*Every good and perfect gift is from above,
coming down from the Father of the heavenly lights,
who does not change like shifting shadows.*
JAMES 1:17 NIV

*A family had given up meat for Lent.
Their three-year-old son said grace for them at dinner one night.
He prayed, "Dear Lord, please bless this food.
God, thank You for our vegetables.
In Your name we pray, amen."*

James says all that God gives us is good and perfect. Whatever we have, God has given to us. Whatever we don't have, we don't need. The problem arises when we become fixated on what we don't have. Then, instead of appreciating what we *do* have, we get irritable; we begin to covet, resulting in a feeling of dissatisfaction. In that scenario, our focus is not upon our abundance from God but upon what we perceive as our lack. But God wants us to be *blessed*, which means "happy." So, instead of being ungrateful, be thankful, recognizing that God blesses us every day. Be content and happy with what you have, realizing how much better off you are than many other people in this world. As we focus on what we have instead of on what we don't have, we will be too busy thanking God for His blessings to get ourselves all frazzled. Realize true joy as you focus on God, the giver of good and perfect gifts.

If we're not thankful for our food before we even get to the table, we can't fool God by saying grace.

THANKFUL EACH MOMENT

See then that you walk circumspectly, not as fools but as wise,
redeeming the time, because the days are evil.
EPHESIANS 5:15–16 NKJV

When told that it was her bedtime,
a seven-year-old said to her babysitter,
"I feel a staying-up-late coming on."

Maybe we feel that this world has stayed up too late, lasted too long in its imperfect condition. Part of us may hope that Jesus comes soon. In the meantime, we can be thankful that God is in control. We know the days are evil. The Bible predicted that there will always be a war going on somewhere and that earthquakes, famines, and floods will happen. Although it may be scary to look around us and see what terrible shape our world is in, God has given us jobs to do. We are here to make the most of the time He has given us, by living the way He wants us to, by loving friend and foe. Thank God that Jesus finished His work on Calvary—not only saving us from our sins but also conquering evil once and for all. Because of Him, we have nothing to worry about. In every situation, adversity as well as prosperity, praise God. We are in His care, today, tomorrow, and on the other side of this earthly life. It's all good!

We are not overcome with evil.
God has overcome evil with His good.

PERCEPTIONS

In everything give thanks;
for this is the will of God in Christ Jesus for you.
1 THESSALONIANS 5:18 NKJV

At a preschool the smell of burnt popcorn hung in the air.
"That's an awful smell," a teacher said.
"No," said a three-year-old boy, "that's dinner."

Naturally, when that boy's mother heard what her son had said, she was mortified. She was a very good cook and had never burnt his dinner. Sometimes we don't know why our children say some of the things they say. But even if we did burn dinner or had a recipe go awry, we can still thank God for it. To keep us from getting discouraged, He helps us make the most out of any situation, delighting in us when we stick in there and do the best we can. Thank God for keeping us in His care 24-7! Although it's a wonderful tradition to celebrate the Thanksgiving holiday every year, we don't want to limit our thanks to God to just one day out of 365. According to the Bible, thanksgiving is an all day, every day sacrifice of praise to our God. That should be our perception, too. Make each day a day of thanksgiving, praising God for His continuous care, no matter how that evening's dinner turns out.

God deserves thanks for everything,
because He does everything for us.

LOCATION

LORD, You have been our dwelling place in all generations.
PSALM 90:1 NKJV

A mother came into the living room and found
her four-year-old son talking on the phone.
She heard him say, "Where do you live, Mr. Man?"
Taking the phone away from her son, the mother apologized
to the person on the other end and hung up. "What were you
doing on the phone?" the mother asked her son.
"You know you're not allowed to call people."
"I wasn't calling anyone," her son protested.
"I was trying to play 'Jingle Bells' on the buttons,
and that man started talking to me."

The world is full of different types of houses, from cabins to castles. If we have any kind of roof over our heads and a place to sleep in safety, we are truly blessed. In many parts of the world, including America, homeless people live desperate lives. We can show our thanks to God by helping the destitute whenever and wherever we can. While some cities have missions that feed their homeless, many churches also have programs to help the needy in their communities. Instead of taking our homes for granted, we need to share our blessings. In the book of Acts, the Christians in some cities took up collections of money to help believers in other cities, particularly in Jerusalem where the Christians were especially poor. This is a wonderful example for us to follow.

No matter where we live, we can open our eyes and hearts
to the needy people of this world.

True Value

The directions the Lord gives are true.
All of them are completely right.
They are more priceless than gold.
They have greater value than huge amounts of pure gold.
PSALM 19:9–10 NIrV

A four-year-old boy told his friend,
"I have a million dollars in my piggy bank."

Sometimes we might dream of what we would do with a million dollars. But money is only money. It has its purposes and it certainly comes in handy. However, as the saying goes, "Money can't buy you happiness." Nor can it buy a lot of other important things. In Acts, Simon the Sorcerer asked Peter to sell him the ability to lay hands on people and have the Holy Spirit come upon them. Peter said to him, "Your money perish with you, because you thought that the gift of God could be purchased with money!" (Acts 8:20 NKJV). God's gifts are just that—gifts. We can't pay Him for them. And one of the gifts God gives us is the benefit of His direction, which is more valuable than great amounts of gold. We think of something as valuable by looking at how much it cost. God's direction to us comes with the greatest cost of all—His only begotten Son. Jesus died and rose again not only to save us from our sins, but to give us the chance to become God's children and to follow Him.

Thank God He loves us enough
to give us His valuable direction.

Our Superhero

*He is the sole expression of the glory of God [the Light-being,
the out-raying or radiance of the divine], and He is the perfect
imprint and very image of [God's] nature, upholding and maintaining
and guiding and propelling the universe by His mighty word of power.
When He had by offering Himself accomplished
our cleansing of sins and riddance of guilt,
He sat down at the right hand of the divine Majesty on high.*
HEBREWS 1:3 AMP

*A five-year-old boy excitedly told his aunt,
"I have Superman underwear."
Then he pulled down his pants to let her see.*

We grow up reading or watching movies about superheroes. We admire their strength and their zeal for justice. We applaud when they outwit the villains. Sometimes we might wish that we were superheroes. Amazingly enough, not only do we know the greatest Superhero of them all—Christ—but we get to be called by His name. Our Superhero never fails. He can walk through walls; change water into wine; heal the leper, the blind, and the crippled; and even walk on water! The villain never gets the best of Him. And Jesus' zeal for justice never ends. His efforts on our behalf are tireless and continuous. Do we ever stop and thank Him for all that He has done for us? Do we appreciate His sacrifice on Calvary? Do we praise Him for conquering death so that we can live with Him forever? Do we tell others about our Superhero? There is none like Him, nor could there ever be. He's the mightiest of the mighty!

Jesus is the only Hero worthy of hero worship.

"Four and a Whole"

Praise the LORD! For it is good to sing praises to our God;
for it is pleasant, and praise is beautiful.
PSALM 147:1 NKJV

A father said to his son,
"It's hard to believe that you're four and a half."
His son indignantly replied,
"I'm not four and a half, I'm four and a whole."

When our children are babies, we count their ages in months. As they get older, we count their ages in whole years, quarter years, and half years. But as *we* get older, we begin counting our own ages in "arounds," saying things like "I'm around forty." We no longer want to be specific. One third-grade girl came home and proudly handed her mother a piece of paper with numbers on it. In math that day, the girl had calculated her mother's age in minutes. Her mother was less than thrilled. But whatever age we are, it's the age God wants us to be right this minute. It is part of who we are right now. Let's thank God for who we are and what we are, recognizing that every age has its own unique joys and discoveries. Praise Him for letting us live in His service. Keep your eyes open, looking forward to the future blessings God has in store for you.

God is the God of every age.

"Good Appletite"

A cheerful heart is good medicine.
PROVERBS 17:22 NIV

A three-year-old boy enjoyed eating apples
so much that he ate them every day.
When his grandmother came to visit, he told her,
"Granny, I love eating apples. I have a good appletite."

It's been said that "an apple a day keeps the doctor away." But Proverbs 17:22 recommends a cheerful heart. Having one will do good like medicine. There was once a woman who had battled cancer for years. Through thick and thin, she kept a cheerful heart. Her attitude of gratitude was an inspiration and a blessing to everyone who knew her. People would come to her for comfort, and she always had some to give. Her family, her church, her neighbors, and the people she worked with were all impressed with her wonderful manner. After ten years, the cancer had spread to the point where it was evident that her time here on earth was coming to an end. Someone said to her, "Are you afraid to die?" The woman laughed and said, "You call it dying; I call it being totally healed." Even if we don't have good health here on earth, we will have perfect health in heaven.

Whatever our circumstance, a cheerful heart will help.

Face-to-Face

For now we see through a glass, darkly; but then face to face: now I know in part; but then shall I know even as also I am known.
1 CORINTHIANS 13:12 KJV

*"I don't need my sunglasses,"
a three-year-old girl told her grandmother.
"My eyes aren't hot."*

We may not be physically blind but our spiritual eyes might need God's light. In the verse above Paul says that we see spiritual things as though looking through a dark glass. Like sunglasses, a dark glass will dim the light. But when we get to heaven we will see God face-to-face. Fanny Crosby was born blind. During her lifetime, she wrote many hymns. In one of them, entitled "Saved by Grace," she wrote, "And I shall see Him face to face." She knew that in heaven she would be blind no longer. Neither will we. Our spiritual darkness will disappear in the light of His presence. And we won't need sunglasses because even though Jesus is the Bright and Morning Star, He will give us spiritual eyes to behold Him. Thank God this world is not our home. All the limitations we have here are temporary. And all our pain here will fade away when we get to heaven. Both facts give us great cause for rejoicing. In the meantime, we can ask God to open our spiritual eyes so that we can learn as much about Jesus as we possibly can here on this earth.

We can be thankful that nothing on earth will grieve us in heaven.

BLESSINGS

CREATURES GREAT AND SMALL

Now the LORD God had formed out of the ground
all the wild animals and all the birds in the sky.
He brought them to the man to see what he would name them;
and whatever the man called each living creature, that was its name.
GENESIS 2:19 NIV

A five-year-old boy asked his mother,
"Mom, is a skunk the same size as a cat?"
The mother answered, "Yes, approximately."
The boy then asked, "What about a wide mouth bass?"

One of the many blessings that God has given us to enjoy is all the wonderful and different creatures He created on this earth. Many people enjoy fishing—not just for the joy of catching a fish, but also for the serene peace of sitting in a boat on the water and enjoying God's scenery. Some are blessed by hearing a bird's song; looking at the elegance of a lion or tiger; or watching the adorable antics of baby animals—puppies, kittens, bear cubs. One woman was suddenly blessed with eleven kittens when her two female cats gave birth within a week of each other. The woman's friends asked her what she was going to do with all those kittens and she replied, "Enjoy them." When the time came, a friend of that woman helped her find good homes for all those precious balls of fur. So the kittens went off to make other people happy. Thank God for blessing us with His love and all creatures, great and small.

When we're counting our blessings,
let's not forget all of God's creatures.

STRETCHING

And Jesus grew in wisdom and stature,
and in favor with God and man.
LUKE 2:52 NIV

A five-year-old boy told his father,
"When I stretch my neck, it makes my head further from the floor."

Part of growing entails stretching our physical muscles. As we grow in Christ, we stretch our spiritual muscles; we exercise our faith, hope, and love. We experience God's grace. We become more and more aware of how God blesses us every day. As we become more spiritually mature, God uses us to bless others. He also helps us to stretch our muscles with "blessings in disguise." While in the midst of difficult situations, we may not recognize them as blessings, but in retrospect, we can see all the good that God brought out of those circumstances. Thank God for giving us the spiritual strength to get through and overcome trials. Whether we are going through a difficult situation now or have just come out of one, we can work out our faith muscles by looking at the Bible and reading about all of God's awesome acts. When we see what He has done in the past, we have more faith to believe in what we know He is going to do in the future. God has never failed us, and He never will.

God has blessed us in the past,
and He has future blessings awaiting us.

Showers of Blessing

*When looking at a picture of a moon rover,
a five-year-old boy asked his father, "Where's the umbrella?
They have meteor showers on Mars, so it needs an umbrella."*

Because we like to be prepared for any and all contingencies, there are many tangible things we think we need to persevere through life. Other times, we just want God to show us a way to escape from a difficult situation. While in the storms of life we can't see how God is using those situations to create blessings for us and for others. In the midst of those trials, other people are watching us, especially if they know we are Christians. When they see how we behave during hard times, they want to know our secret. That's our opportunity to tell them about how wonderful God is and how He can make good come out of anything. Although we might pray to be delivered from our troubles, God knows we will benefit more by going through them, knowing He will never give us more trouble than we can stand. When we allow Him to work His perfect will, the blessings He bestows on us are always more than we ever dreamed of. So relax. Let go and let God. He's got everything under control—through the sunshine and the showers.

*When God is showering us with blessings,
we don't want to be holding up an umbrella.*

WEASELS

The LORD God formed a man from the dust of the ground and
breathed into his nostrils the breath of life,
and the man became a living being.
GENESIS 2:7 NIV

A three-year-old boy saw an older man who was having trouble
breathing. As the man took in air from his oxygen tank, he made a
wheezing noise. Later the boy asked his mother, "What was that noise
that man made?" "It's called wheezing," his mother explained.
"It's what happens when you're having trouble breathing."
The boy said nothing more about it.
When his father got home from work that night, the boy greeted
him with, "I saw a man with weasels today."

Most of us tend to take breathing for granted. Unless we have
an episode of choking or have a bad cold where our breathing
is restricted, we take no notice of this, not just daily but every
single second of the day, blessing. But what about our spiritual
breathing? God breathed into us His breath of life, His Spirit.
It lives in us daily. Are we taking Him for granted as much as
we take our own breathing for granted? When we are physically
agitated, sometimes taking deep breaths can calm us down.
When we are spiritually agitated, deep breaths of God's Holy
Spirit will cover us with His peace.

What a blessing that the Creator of the universe
wants to be as vital to us as breathing is to our bodies.

"OLD MAIDY"

*"Observe how the lilies of the field grow. . .I say to you that not even
Solomon in all his glory clothed himself like one of these.
But if God so clothes the grass of the field,
which is alive today and tomorrow is thrown into the furnace,
will He not much more clothe you?"*

MATTHEW 6:28–30 NASB

*A grandmother said to her granddaughter,
"What a pretty dress."
"Yes," replied the three-year-old proudly,
"we got it at Old Maidy [Old Navy]."*

Some people are exceedingly proud of their wardrobe, seeing it
as a status symbol. They only wear designer labels and make sure
everyone knows where they got their outfits. God has promised
to give us what we need, which includes clothing. But He didn't
promise to give us expensive designer clothes. Instead He asks
us to consider how He clothes the lilies of the field and to use
that knowledge to increase our faith in His willingness and
ability to supply our necessities. Since He has blessed us with
all that we need, maybe we should look in our closets and see if
we have anything there we can use to bless someone else. Many
churches have resource centers where they take used clothing
and distribute it to the homeless in their area. As God has
blessed us, so we can use His blessings to bless others.

**The only designer label we need to be clothed in
is the righteousness of God.**

The Blessing of Marriage

Her children rise up and call her blessed;
her husband also, and he praises her.
PROVERBS 31:28 NKJV

A seven-year-old girl told her mother,
"I know what Snow White's last name is. White."
The mother decided to tease her daughter and said with a smile,
"If Snow White's last name is White then why
is her sister named Rose Red?"
Shrugging, the seven-year-old said, "Maybe she's married."

One of the greatest blessings God has given His people is marriage. It has been said that Adam is the only man in the world who went to sleep and woke up married. From the beginning God knew how helpful it would be for the man to have a partner equal yet different from him. Not only is a good marriage a blessing to the partners involved, but it is an even bigger blessing to any children who may come as a result of this union. Our children learn most of their behaviors at home. When their home environment is loving, nurturing, and spiritual, that is what they will consider normal and emulate. When they see the pattern of a good marriage enacted before them, then their desire will be to have such a relationship of their own. Too many marriages are dissolved these days because the people involved were never taught how to make and maintain this special relationship. We can show the world what God intended marriage to be. In doing so, we will also be training our children so that they, too, can show their generation when the time comes.

Let us be a blessing to our spouses and our children.

Speaking God's Blessing

"The LORD bless you and keep you; the LORD make
his face shine on you and be gracious to you;
the LORD turn his face toward you and give you peace."
NUMBERS 6:24-26 NIV

A woman was visiting her brother's family.
While there, she offered to go to their grocery store
and get some things her sister-in-law needed for supper.
The woman's six-year-old niece offered to go to the store with her.
When they got there, the niece told her aunt proudly,
"I know this store like the back of my head."
(And she was right—she couldn't find anything.)

Speaking through Moses, God told Aaron and his sons to bless Israel, using the words in the verses above. Thousands of years later, these words apply to and bless us! How awesome that God meets us face-to-face. Not only that, He makes His face to shine upon us. God blesses us with His peace that surpasses all understanding. Because words are powerful, God wanted this blessing spoken. When was the last time you spoke a blessing into someone's life? "Have a blessed day" is a wonderful way to greet family, friends, and even strangers! Although we may feel uncomfortable blessing someone with words, that's how God blesses us. So share the happiness—bless someone else with your words today!

Our speech can bless others. Pass it on!

Blessing and Cursing

Out of the same mouth proceed blessing and cursing.
My brethren, these things ought not to be so.
JAMES 3:10 NKJV

When caught eavesdropping, an eight-year-old told her mother,
"It's not my fault. I heard you overtalking."

It is said eavesdroppers rarely hear anything good about themselves. Keeping that in mind, we need to be careful about what we say. People are listening, and so is God. And He is the only one who can bring blessing out of cursing. When Balaam was asked by Balak, king of Moab, to come curse the children of Israel, God told him not to go. But Balaam went anyway. On the way, the Angel of the Lord appeared to tell Balaam that he was only to speak what the Lord told him to say. When Balaam got to Moab, King Balak took him up on a mountain so that he could overlook the children of Israel. But instead of cursing them, Balaam blessed them. Aghast, King Balak couldn't believe his ears. "What have you done?" he asked Balaam. "I asked you to curse my enemies and you have blessed them bountifully" (see Numbers 23:11–12). King Balak thought maybe the location was the problem. So he took Balaam to two more places and twice more Balaam blessed the Israelites. Finally, Balak said, "If you won't curse them, at least quit blessing them!" But Balaam told him again that he had to speak what the Lord told him to say. Balak angrily departed and Balaam went back home. (See Numbers 22–24).

Let us bless instead of curse.

HOLIDAYS

One Mother's Day, Alice was visiting her daughter Joan when
the phone rang. It was Alice's other daughter, Mary,
calling to wish her mother a happy Mother's Day.
Then Mary put her son, Chuck, on the phone to extend the same
holiday greeting. Chuck had been pestering his mother
all day to let him talk to his cousin, Joan's son, Allen. When Chuck got
on the phone he said in a rush, "Happy Mother's Day, Grandma.
Will you put Allen on the phone?"

To some people, any and all holidays—from New Year's Day and Christmas to Saint Patrick's Day and President's Day— are a cause for celebration. To others, holidays are silly and to be avoided. Then there are those who dread holidays—such as Easter, Thanksgiving, and Christmas—because of all the stress involved in preparations for and obligatory attendance at family gatherings. Fortunately, our God gives us the choice to decide what days and events we want to celebrate and how we want to celebrate them, for all our holidays are blessings from Him. Some people think there is no need to have special days to celebrate God's blessings—that we can celebrate them every day. That is true. But whether we commemorate special days or not, we are all partakers of God's blessings and that makes every day special.

God blesses us with the gift of choice
and then gives us wonderful choices to make.

"NUFFY"

May the Lord give you understanding in all things.
2 TIMOTHY 2:7 NKJV

A father was sitting on the sofa, watching TV, when his four-year-old daughter came into the room. She was having trouble breathing through her nose because she had a cold.
"What's the matter, sweetheart?" the father asked.
"I'm all nuffy," his daughter replied.

Sometimes we may feel like we have a spiritual cold, as if our spiritual understanding is all stopped up. But God has blessed us with His Spirit. *Pneuma*, the Greek word for "Spirit" can also be translated "a current of air" or "breath." God is our spiritual air. He can and will open our understanding of the things He wants to teach us. But sometimes we have to read the same scripture over and over to get its meaning. In the same way we breathe air in and out to say alive physically, God wants us to repeatedly "inhale" His Word so that His Spirit can give us spiritual life. With all the many blessings God gives us each and every day, there are always more to be had. Reading God's Word not only points out blessings we may have overlooked, but God says just reading His Word will bless and inspire us (see 2 Timothy 3:16–17). We don't have to be "nuffy." We can take in the refreshing Spirit of God's Word and as we do, He blesses us with the fullness of His joy.

Breathing is as valuable as God's Word. Both are blessings.

COMMUNICATION

"Bye"

Are not two little sparrows sold for a penny?
And yet not one of them will fall to the ground
without your Father's leave (consent) and notice.
MATTHEW 10:29 AMP

A mother was very concerned when her family's pet bird got sick
because her six-year-old daughter was very attached to it.
They took their pet to the vet, but the bird died.
So they brought their feathered friend home
to give it a funeral in their backyard.
Right before they put the bird into the ground,
the mother said to her daughter,
"Did you want to say anything?"
The daughter looked at the bird and said, "Bye."

Anyone who has ever had a pet pass away knows the sorrow that it causes, especially for our children. But Matthew 10:29 tells us that God loves all His creations so much that even a sparrow cannot die without Him noticing. And He loves *us* so much more than sparrows! Because of that great love, God comforts us in our sorrows so that we can know what true comfort is. The result of that is that we now have the comfort of God to share with others in distress (see 2 Corinthians 1:3–4). How wonderful to know that we are not alone, that God—whose Son was called a "Man of sorrows. . .acquainted with grief" (Isaiah 53:3 NKJV)—knows what we are going through, sympathizes, and continuously pours His love upon us. Now that's comfort!

He who sees the sparrows fall will hear our call.

Describing the Indescribable

*Blessed is the one who reads the words of this prophecy.
Blessed are those who hear it and think everything it says is
important. The time when these things will come true is near.*
REVELATION 1:3 NIrV

*Having only ever had boneless chicken,
a four-year-old boy was excitedly telling his mother
about the chicken on a bone that he had had at his neighbor's house.
"I don't know what it was," he said, "but it looked like the letter I."
(It was a drumstick.)*

Some people think the book of Revelation—filled with descriptions of things we can't even imagine—is difficult to understand. But the first verse tells us what Revelation is really about—it is Jesus revealing Himself to us. Just like the parables Jesus told His disciples, the book of Revelation is a mystery for us to study and, with the help of God's Spirit, to understand. God deliberately speaks to us in signs and symbols and parables because He wants us to concentrate on what He is telling us. The more effort we put into comprehending God's message, the closer we come to God Himself. God wants to reveal Himself to us, but He wants us to be willing to accept His revelations. What a wonderful God we have! The Creator of the universe wants to make Himself known to us. We are fortunate people indeed.

God reveals Himself to us every day.

Speaking Truth

These are the things you shall do:
Speak each man the truth to his neighbor.
ZECHARIAH 8:16 NKJV

A family was making preparations for
a visit from a student from France.
When the mother announced that
their guest would be arriving the next day,
her thirteen-year-old daughter said, "Oh, good.
I'll brush up on my Spanish."
(Note: the exchange student didn't speak Spanish either.)

Sometimes the hardest thing we can do is speak the truth. It can almost seem like a foreign language to us. Some people feel it's okay to tell "social lies." By that they mean that if someone asks you if you like her outfit and you don't want to hurt her feelings, you lie and say that you like it, even if you don't. But there are many ways to tell the truth without hurting someone's feelings. As always, Jesus is our example in this regard. When He was talking to the woman at the well, He told her to go and get her husband. When she said that she didn't have one, He said, "You have well said that you have no husband because the one you have now isn't yours" (see John 4:18). Instead of being insulted, she was awed. It takes more creativity to tell the truth than to lie. When our boss doesn't want to be disturbed, instead of lying and saying he isn't there, we can say that he's not available. There are always alternatives to lying.

Telling the truth is a choice.

"Kissy Poo"

The hearing ear and the seeing eye, the LORD has made them both.
PROVERBS 20:12 NKJV

In a store, a four-year-old boy began insisting
that he wanted a "kissy poo."
When his mother asked him to show her one, he pointed to a kazoo.

Sometimes just hearing something isn't enough. To understand what we've heard, we need to see it. God knows this and He gives us all kinds of visual aids—for our physical eyes and our spiritual eyes. When God wanted to show us how much He loves and understands us, He gave us the greatest sight of all— Jesus! In Jesus we can see that God truly does understand us because He became *like* us. Along with giving us ears to hear and eyes to see, God gave us lessons to learn. The greatest lesson of all is that, because God wants us to know Him, He reveals Himself to us in every way He can. We have the heavens declaring His glory. We have the stars singing His praises with joy. We have all aspects of Him in the people He surrounds us with. We have our children and their innocent God-given wisdom. We have the stories of how God loved and treated His people in the past. God does everything He can to show us who He is. We need to look and listen for Him everywhere.

We can be visual aids to the people around us
so they, too, can see God.

"Not Deaf"

People were overwhelmed with amazement.
"He has done everything well," they said.
"He even makes the deaf hear and the mute speak."
MARK 7:37 NIV

A six-year-old girl was very proud of her new ability to read.
As she and her family traveled in their car,
the girl read all the road signs they passed.
When she misread one sign, her eight-year-old brother corrected her.
Indignantly, the girl said, "I can read, John! I'm not deaf!"

When Jesus made the deaf hear, He didn't just heal those who were physically deaf. He opened the spiritual ears of the people so they could hear His message. Crowds followed Him around because they couldn't get enough of His teachings. Acts 2 says that on Pentecost, three thousand souls were added to the church. This is in addition to the ones who were already disciples. Where did all those people come from? Most likely some of them were the ones who had followed Jesus around, listening to Him. Their spiritual ears were opened. So when Peter preached his sermon on Pentecost, they were ready to hear him and to act upon his message. We might sometimes become spiritually deaf. Maybe not completely deaf but certainly hard of hearing. We fail to hear the cries of the needy around us. We fail to hear a lost world's call of "Come help us." We fail to hear God's clear instructions about how we are to live our lives. But spending time with God and reading His word will open our spiritual ears once more.

Thank God we're not spiritually deaf!

"Not the Day to Mess with Me"

Our Lord Jesus is the great Shepherd of the sheep.
The God who gives peace brought him back from the dead.
He did it because of the blood of the eternal covenant. May God
supply you with everything good. Then you can do what he wants.
May he do in us what is pleasing to him. We can do it only with the
help of Jesus Christ. Give him glory for ever and ever. Amen.
HEBREWS 13:20-21 NIrV

A four-year-old girl was misbehaving.
Her mother told her that if she didn't start behaving properly,
she would end up in time-out. The little girl said to her mother,
"This is not the day to mess with me. I am not in the mood."
Startled at hearing her own words coming out of her daughter's mouth,
the mother at first couldn't think of any reply.
Then she said, "Mood or not, you have to behave,"
and then gave her daughter a time-out.

There is an old saying, "Little pitchers have big ears." Indeed our children hear what we say. But they usually hear the things we don't want them to hear—and completely miss the things we *do* want them to hear. How many times have we heard our children repeat something we've said? According to the verse above, we have a powerful ally who can produce in us all that is pleasing to Him. If we take the time to think about what we are going to say then ask God for His input, we won't be so apt to say negative things that our children will pick up. Someone once said, "If you wouldn't write it down and sign your name to it then you shouldn't say it." Very good advice.

Our words need to be positive, not negative.

Giving a Reason

*Always be prepared to give an answer to everyone who asks you
to give a reason for the hope that you have.*
1 Peter 3:15 NIV

*A seven-year-old girl who was supposed to
be in bed came into the living room.
"Why are you up?" her mother asked her.
"I have to tell you something important,"
the girl replied. When the child just stood there,
her mother prompted her, "Well, what is it?"
The girl looked up at the ceiling and said, "Um. . . Um. . ."
"That's what I thought," the mother said. "Go back to bed."*

When someone asks us how we can live in this world and still
be hopeful, we shouldn't let the question catch us unaware.
We don't want to be standing around saying, "Um. . . Um. . ." In
the verse above, Peter tells us that we need to be so sure of what
we believe and in whom we believe so that when anyone asks
us a reason for the hope we have, we can answer immediately.
The answer is God. No one can live in this world and have hope
without Him. There are some people who claim that they don't
believe in God or in His existence. This leads us to wonder how
they cope with their lives. Who can live without hope? And
who can have hope without God?

**God is our hope, our rock, and our salvation.
Praise be to God!**

On the Same Page

Having been perfected, He became
the author of eternal salvation to all who obey Him...
of whom we have much to say, and hard to explain,
since you have become dull of hearing.
HEBREWS 5:9, 11 NKJV

Finding, then reading a letter she had written
to her seven-year-old son when he was a baby,
a mother became overwhelmed by emotion.
When her son came into the room, she said, "Listen to this letter
I wrote to you right after you were born."
She began reading the letter aloud, and when she was through,
her son looked at her and said,
"Can we have chicken for supper?"

How many times have we said things to our children and then reprimanded them for not listening to us? In the verses above, the writer of Hebrews was reprimanding the people he was writing to because they weren't listening to him. The phrase "dull of hearing" is a very interesting description. Proverbs 27:17 says: "As iron sharpens iron, so one person sharpens another" (NIV). This can pertain to how we communicate our understanding of God's Word. As one of us receives an insight, we share it with others, and they in turn share their insights with us. This is how we become sharp instead of "dull of hearing." There may be certain biblical topics of which we think we know all there is to know. But then someone else shows us a whole new meaning, and we discover an aspect that we never considered before.

Learning about God is an ongoing experience.

"TALK TO THE HAND"

Two four-year-old girls were having an argument.
The first one held up her hand and said, "Talk to the hand."
The second girl said, "Hand? Hand? It's not talking back!"

Fortunately for us, every time we talk to God, He listens to us. He is never too busy. He never ignores us. But do we listen in return?

Who has time in this whirling world
To hear the still, small voice of the Lord?
"Please speak louder," I prayed, "when You speak to me."
God replied, "Stand still and be quiet. Listen to Me."

Prayer is not just a one-sided conversation. After talking to God, we need to listen to His reply. God told Isaiah that He was calling to His people, "Here I am, here I am" (Isaiah 65:1 NIV), and no one would listen. We don't want to ignore God's call to us. He is always there for us. We need to always be there for Him. It should break our hearts to think of God calling out, "Here I am," and hear no one respond. Let's answer God's call as Samuel did: "Speak, for your servant hears."

A life of communication with God will give us great advantage.

WET CAT

Do not provoke your children to wrath,
but bring them up in the training and admonition of the Lord.
EPHESIANS 6:4 NKJV

A nanny was teaching a five-year-old girl to read some words.
When they came to the word wet,
the five year old couldn't remember it.
Trying to give her a hint, the nanny said,
"If you throw water on a cat, what does the cat get?"
"Mad," replied the little girl.

We are to be a positive influence in our children's lives. Instead of boxing them in with a bunch of negative rules, we are to teach them in the same manner God teaches us—with positive leadership. Our children are going to get frustrated and irritated as they grow up, but we can avoid deliberately provoking them. Instead of a bunch of "don'ts," we can teach them God's "dos." The biggest one of God's "dos" is the Golden Rule: "Do to others as you would have them do to you" (Luke 6:31 NIV). This applies to us as parents, too. We should do to our children as we would have liked our parents to do to us. We won't be able to avoid using the word *no*. God says no to us many times. But we can give a reason for the *no* so that our children understand we have their well being at heart and are not just being mean. Above all, we should let them know every day how very much we love them.

Loving our children means training them up
in the way God wants them to go.

"WHAT DID THE BANANA SAY?"

*"Does the LORD delight in burnt offerings and sacrifices as much
as in obeying the LORD? To obey is better than sacrifice."*
1 SAMUEL 15:22 NIV

*When asked by his older brother,
"What did the banana say to the monkey?"
a four-year-old boy replied, "Nothing. Bananas can't talk."*

God gives us clear and specific instructions. We need to take them literally. Through the prophet Samuel, God told Saul, king of the Israelites, to totally annihilate the Amalekites by destroying the people and everything they owned, including all their livestock. When Saul reported his success to Samuel, Saul said that he had done everything the Lord had commanded him to do. And right at that moment, a sheep bleated, making a liar out of him. When Samuel confronted Saul about this lack of complete obedience, Saul excused himself by blaming it on his troops, saying they had saved some sheep and oxen to sacrifice to the Lord, and had pressured Saul into obeying them. According to the verse above, we cannot please God in our own way or by caving in to pressure from others. We only please Him when we do things His way. We can't always see the results of our disobedience. But because Saul didn't kill the king of the Amalekites, Agag, like God commanded, some Amalekites were left alive. We all know one of Agag's descendants—his name is Haman and, during the time of Esther, he did all he could to kill all the Jews.

**We need to obey the Lord completely because we love Him.
He alone can see the consequences of disobedience.**

What Did You Say?

Let wise people listen and add to what they have learned.
PROVERBS 1:5 NIrV

*A three-year-old boy asked his grandmother to put
"cute numbers" (cucumbers) on his salad.*

Often when our children are talking, our listening becomes
not just hearing the words they are saying but endeavoring to
understand what they are *trying* to say. When two people are
talking, four things are taking place at exactly the same time.
There is what the first person actually says and what she meant
to say, and there is what the second person actually hears and
what she thinks she hears. So there is room for interpretation.
This is how rumors get started. Someone repeats what she
thinks she heard another say, which, if erroneous, can often lead
to strife. True listening means paying attention to and trying
to understand the meaning of what someone is telling us. This
isn't always easy. That's why we ask questions. "What did you
say?" "What did you mean?" "Did I understand you correctly?"
Obviously there will be some miscommunication at times. But
we need to make sure that we are doing our best to avoid it by
listening with our intelligence and not just with our ears. The
key to communicating with others is for us to express ourselves
as clearly as possible and then to listen to what someone else
says as closely as possible.

We can't just hear we have to listen.

WHISPERING

A whisperer separates the best of friends.
PROVERBS 16:28 NKJV

A three-year-old boy told his mother, "I want to whisper in your ear."
Then he put his ear next to her ear and proceeded to whisper.

In the Bible, whispering is often associated with gossip and talebearing. "Whisper Down the Lane" illustrates how easily words gets misunderstood and misinterpreted. In that game, the first person whispers a sentence to the person next to them. The second person then whispers what he thinks he heard to the next person in line. When the last person has heard the sentence, she says it out loud. Often what she says bears no resemblance at all to the original sentence. When we repeat something that we've heard, we run the risk of not getting it correct, of spreading a story that isn't true. Whispering is also associated with sneakiness. In movies, the villains whisper to each other so their plots won't be overheard by the good guys. We don't want to be sneaky. We want to be open and aboveboard. We don't want to separate friends but be the promoters of unity. If and when we do whisper, let us be sure to comfort others with our words, as in the hymn "Whispering Hope."

Instead of being whisperers,
let us gladly proclaim the good news of great joy.

CORRECTING OTHERS

"Why do you look at the speck of sawdust in your brother's eye and pay no attention to the plank in your own eye? . . . First take the plank out of your eye, and then you will see clearly to remove the speck from your brother's eye."

LUKE 6:41–42 NIV

A three-year-old girl announced, "I want yogret."
"It's not yogret," her three-year-old cousin corrected her.
"It's 'ogurt!"

The verses above are actually very humorous. Can you imagine someone walking around with a piece of lumber sticking out of her eye? Now, can you visualize her trying to remove a speck from her neighbor's eye? The plank would actually stop her from getting close enough to even *see* the speck in her neighbor's eye, much less try to remove it. A Pennsylvania Dutch proverb says, "Our faults irritate us most when we see them in others." It's true! The huge plank of our own imperfections blinds us to the goodness in others. Luke 6:42 tells us to get the plank out of our own eye, to deal with correcting our own faults before trying to help someone else. Doing so may keep us too busy to ever attempt to correct another person. In any case, once God has removed our imperfections, whittling away at them bit by bit, only then may we see clearly enough, be worthy enough, to offer an eye wash to someone else.

We are to see others as God sees them—
as His children—and not focus on their faults.

"You Democrat!"

Let the words of my mouth and the meditation of my heart be acceptable in Your sight, O LORD, my rock and my Redeemer.
PSALM 19:14 NASB

A four-year-old girl was very angry with her cousin. Having been raised in a very political household, she called him the worst name she could think of—"You Democrat!"

We might smile at this, but name-calling is a sin. God isn't as much concerned with the words we use as He is with the emotions behind them. We're supposed to love each other, not be angry and call each other names. Yes, people have and will continue to make us mad. When they say things that irritate or hurt us, our first reaction might be retaliation. But God says that vengeance is His. Why? Because every action has an equal and opposite reaction. We might not know what we're setting in motion by retaliating against someone, but God does. When it comes to vengeance, only He can handle the fallout. We can't. Anger begets more anger. Love begets more love. Although we don't always know the reasons behind why someone is mean to us, God does. He knows the person's heart. So leave it to God and forgive like Jesus, our example in all things. He didn't allow the horrible things done or said to Him affect His love for all of us. "Father, forgive them; for they know not what they do" (Luke 23:34 KJV).

We can forgive because Jesus forgave us.

DISCIPLINE

ACTING IN

Let all things be done decently and in order.
1 CORINTHIANS 14:40 NKJV

A babysitter said to her four-year-old charge,
"I've never seen you acting out like this before."
"What is acting out?" the little girl asked.
"Behaving badly," the babysitter replied.
The little girl thought a minute, then said,
"I'm behaving goodly now. I'm acting in."

We all want our children to "act in" instead of "out," but how are they seeing us behave? Are we, as Christians, "acting in"? A father took his six-year-old son into the woods with him one winter. There was snow on the ground. After they had gone a short way into the forest, the father realized his son wasn't walking beside him. He turned around, and there was his son carefully stepping into each print the father had made in the snow. Our children follow in our footsteps. They behave as they see us behave. In the verse above, Paul was addressing believers at the church in Corinth. Their services were unruly with members trying to show off their spiritual gifts. Paul told them to use their gifts to edify one another, not to compete, but to do things decently and in order. This is good advice for "all things" in our lives. God wants us to show our children how to behave properly. He wants us to edify our fellow Christians and not compete with them for positions of prestige. Let's provide good examples for our children and "act in."

As we do, so our children will do.

THE KING'S DAUGHTER

The king's daughter is all glorious within.
PSALM 45:13 KJV

A man asked his three-year-old granddaughter
what she wanted to be for Halloween.
"A bat," she replied.
"Don't you want to be a princess?" her grandfather asked.
"Grandpa," the girl said with an exasperated sigh, "I'm a princess
every day. I have to be something different for Halloween."

The literal meaning of the verse above was that the king's daughter, in all her glorious apparel, was inside the house, awaiting her bridegroom. However, we, as the King's daughters, can apply another meaning to this verse. Because we reflect God's glory, we are all glorious within—inside our souls and ourselves. We are Christians every day. We have exchanged the ashes of sin for the beauty of salvation. We wear our salvation as a glorious garment, and its beauty is enhanced by the love of God dwelling in us. Inner beauty is superior to outward beauty. A model at a fashion show was deemed to be one of the most beautiful women in the world. Her looks were flawless, and she carried herself with grace. After the show was over, a reporter tried to get an interview with her. The model screamed curses at him and slammed her dressing room door in his face. Turning to a colleague, the reporter said, "I've heard that she is one of the most beautiful women in the world, but right now she just looks ugly to me." We want our inner beauty to shine forth.

No matter what we look like physically,
we, the King's daughters, are all glorious within.

BEING HONEST

Provide things honest in the sight of all men.
ROMANS 12:17 KJV

A ten-year-old girl's aunt was visiting her for the Christmas holidays. "Do you have any plans for this afternoon?" the aunt asked her niece. "No," said the girl. "I'm just going to stay here and be bored with you."

Sometimes our children say things in all honesty when we wish they wouldn't. Their truthfulness can be like a bright light showing up things we would prefer to keep hidden. But we can never fault our children for being honest. Shakespeare's quote, "Honesty is the best policy," is still true today. Unfortunately, we live in a not-so-honest world where some people believe that being a Christian should not interfere with their shady business practices. Many years ago, when he was a store clerk, Abraham "Honest Abe" Lincoln walked three miles just to return a small sum of money to a woman he had mistakenly overcharged. We want to be like Abe. We want to be honest subjects of God's kingdom. We want our word to be our bond. We want to be dependable and trustworthy. Other people are looking at us to see whether we are living up to God's standards. Are we?

God's wants us to shine the bright light of honesty into the darkness of this dishonest world.

"Being-haved"

*Surely I have behaved and quieted myself, as a child
that is weaned of his mother: my soul is even as a weaned child.*
PSALM 131:2 KJV

A four-year-old boy was watching Disney's Toy Story.
Suddenly he announced to his family, "Woody is not being-haved!"

Behavior is something that we must teach our children because they are born not knowing how to conduct themselves properly. A baby cries whenever it is hungry. But a weaned child, knowing that food is coming, learns to wait until food appears. God wants us to behave like weaned children—not crying for what we want whenever we want it, but waiting patiently, knowing that He will supply our every need. Certainly, we can pray and ask for whatever we desire. And if it is in God's plan for us, He will give it to us. But we should not constantly whine and cry and complain as if we can wear God down so that He'll give us what we want just to hush us up. Obviously a weaned child is more mature than a baby. A weaned child eats meals at the table with the rest of the family at the appointed times. Just so, God has His appointed times when He supplies whatever we need. Dependence upon God is a behavior we spend our lives learning and applying.

**The Lord wants us to depend on Him
just like our children depend on us.**

Complaining

Do all things without complaining and disputing.
PHILIPPIANS 2:14 NKJV

A six-year-old girl told her nanny, "I'm bored."
"Would you like to help me with this housework?" her nanny asked.
"Sure," said the girl. The nanny had her sweep the kitchen floor.
As soon as she was done sweeping, the girl sat down on the floor.
"What's the matter?" asked her nanny.
"All this work is making me tired," the girl replied.

How tired we get of our children's grumbling. Sometimes their complaints are valid. At other times we wish they would just do as they are told without giving us grief about it. But do we do that to God our Father? Do we do what He tells us to do without complaining or arguing? Oftentimes, people gripe about the weather. With all our lessons about the goodness of God, do we have the right to complain about storms, excessive heat, and hurricanes? After all, who is in charge of the climate, the seasons, the sunshine, and the rain? God. After a major thunderstorm, we can hear birds singing away. They aren't complaining; they're celebrating. After the Israelites had been delivered from Egypt, they weren't in the wilderness very long before they started complaining. God gave them manna, quail, the pillar of fire, and the pillar of cloud—and *still* they complained. Not a good example to follow. Instead, praise God for all His great and glorious works. Look for His mighty and awesome hand in everything—without complaint.

When we focus on God, we can see
that we have nothing to complain about.

Do It My Way

*Jesus said to him, "I am the way, the truth, and the life.
No one comes to the Father except through Me."*
JOHN 14:6 NKJV

*An eight–year–old girl was having a slumber party.
After everyone had arrived, she came upstairs and told her mother,
"All of my friends are having a good time
and they're not even doing what I told them."*

Some people think that Christians are too narrow in their thinking. Well, Jesus said that the way that leads to life is narrow (see Matthew 7:14). In fact, He narrowed it down to Himself. *He* is the way—the only way. So we may justly be accused of being narrow for we are in the process of being conformed to one Person. How narrow is that? As we go forward toward Him, we become more like Him. However, we all know people who insist on and expect everyone to do things their way. That's a surefire recipe for their living a miserable life. Fortunately as Christians, we've been given a different roadmap, another path to follow. For our steps are ordered by the Lord and He delights in being our way (see Psalm 37:23). We don't have what it takes to order our own steps. So instead of getting ourselves all worked up trying to make people do things our way, we need to relax, go God's way, and point others to *the* Way.

The only way is Jesus' way.

Keeping the Lid On

On the way to the store a ten-year-old girl was very antsy
in the backseat of the car.
"Put a lid on it," her mother commanded. The girl calmed down.
When they arrived at the store the girl was out of the car and running
across the parking lot before her mother could get out of the car.
"Come back here," the mother called. When the girl returned, her
mother said, "I thought I told you to put a lid on it, and what was
the first thing you did when I stopped the car?"
"Took the lid off," the girl replied.

There are days when we have so much to do we don't know where to start. Sometimes the pressure gets to us and we simply boil over. The verse above says that when God created us, He planned a daily schedule for us. If we are overwhelmed with things to do or complaining about how tired we are, maybe we're doing more than God intended. Although it's sometimes difficult to say no when asked to head a committee or to join a ministry, or to take that extra class, we need to be sure not to overcommit ourselves. Nor should we over-schedule our children. God says His burden is light. It is not His plan to overwhelm us or wear us out.

Instead of telling God what we're going to do,
we need to ask Him what He wants us to do.

Keeping the Rules

*For they bind heavy burdens and grievous to be borne,
and lay them on men's shoulders; but they themselves
will not move them with one of their fingers.*
MATTHEW 23:4 KJV

*Having decided her household needed some rules,
a six-year-old girl came up with the following list:*
1. *No running in the house.*
2. *No skipping in the house.*
3. *Do not be a drama queen.*
4. *Ask when you want a snack.*
5. *Ask when you want to use the phone.*
6. *Ask when you want to pick a flower.*

In the verse above, Jesus was talking to the Pharisees, religious rulers of His day. He found fault with them because they were distorting the law of God. They tried to use their "rules"—their interpretation of God's law—to make other people do as they commanded. There are people today who do what the Pharisees did—they make up their own version of God's law and then lead people astray. The only rules binding on anyone are God's rules. The only one in charge of God's kingdom is God. He doesn't have committees and subcommittees and panels to discuss what His "policy" should be. He has already decided. Psalm 19:8 says: "The statutes of the LORD are right, rejoicing the heart: the commandment of the LORD is pure, enlightening the eyes" (KJV). When we keep the pure law of the Lord, we find joy and direction, for His rules shine light upon our path.

God's rules cause us to rejoice, not to groan.

"Needs a Spanking"

Don't hold back training from a child. If you correct him, he won't die.
So correct him. Then you will save him from death.
PROVERBS 23:13–14 NIrV

Watching a villain on a movie one day,
a four-year-old boy said to his babysitter,
"That man needs a spanking."

Our children know when someone needs corrected—usually someone other than themselves. People may argue over the type of discipline a child should have, but they agree that children should be disciplined. A mother took her three-year-old son to a child psychologist who told her that she was being too negative and should stop saying the word *no* to her son. "Oh, really?" said the woman. "So if he runs out into traffic I should just let him go?" The psychologist had no answer for her. Just like God lovingly disciplines us to keep our souls safe for eternity, we lovingly discipline our children (see Proverbs 13:24) to keep them physically and spiritually safe. By doing so, we will save them from death—physically and spiritually. One of the best ways to keep our children safe is to teach them to hide God's Word in their heart by memorizing verses that will instruct them in the way God wants them to go. God entrusted our children to us. We need to entrust them back to Him.

Everybody may not need a spanking, but we all need discipline.

NOT KNOWING WHAT WE NEED

"Your Father knows that you need these things."
LUKE 12:30 NKJV

*A mother used a "thinking chair" as a discipline tool with her children.
On her son's fifth birthday, he was misbehaving
so she told him that he would have to spend
some time in the thinking chair.
The boy was shocked. "I don't need the thinking chair anymore,"
he protested. "I'm five!"*

As we become more mature in our Christian walk, we might come to think that we know *exactly* what we need. But we must beware that we do not fall into the trap of thinking we must have the material "perks" of this world. We don't need position, possessions, or prosperity to be happy. Although those things are nice and can be used for God's glory, they are not necessary. We also needn't be worried about the necessities of life. All our cares are fruitless and vain. Fretting will only hinder our Christian walk. So we must pay attention to our "self-talk," monitor our minds to prevent their continual seesawing between hope and fear, which will only keep our nerves all knotted up. Cease worrying about necessities, large and small. God has given us all things—not to possess but to enjoy. The birds sing because they don't have to pay taxes, work on their wardrobes, or paint their houses. They simply enjoy what God gives. May we do the same.

We may not know what we need, but God does.

Recognizing the Obvious

"I have loved you," says the LORD.
"Yet you say, 'In what way have You loved us?'"
MALACHI 1:2 NKJV

A class of inattentive kindergarten children was supposed to be
practicing their song for a Christmas pageant. After they had
"sung" the song through once, the teacher admonished them,
"You'll have to sing louder." They went through the song
a second time, and the teacher said, "I still can't hear you."
One of the children said, "It's because we're not singing."

In Malachi 1–3, God carries on an amazing dialogue with His people. He makes a series of statements and they question everything He says. Then God answers their questions in explicit detail. It's as if they are in a courtroom and God is bringing His case to them—not to condemn them but to show them how what they were doing was contrary to His plan for them. All through this dialogue, God keeps repeating how much He loves them then proving it with all kinds of illustrations. One of the things the people were doing was taking blemished animals to the temple for sacrifice. God's law clearly stated that any sacrificial animal was to be without blemish and without spot. God says to His people, "What do you think your governor would say if you gave him a lame or blind or sickly animal as a gift?" (see Malachi 1:6). They had no answer. We can't fool God. He knows what He's done, and He knows what we've done—or haven't done.

God gave us His best. He deserves our best.

Recognizing the Problem

"God be merciful to me a sinner!"
LUKE 18:13 NKJV

A three-year-old girl was misbehaving so
her father made her sit on a chair.
But the child continued to misbehave.
Exasperated, the father said to her, "What is your problem?"
Her five-year-old sister replied, "I think you're her problem, Dad."

In Luke 18:9–14, Jesus tells the story of two men. Both of them had a problem. The Pharisee was a leader in his community. He took pride in his position in life. He went to the temple—not to pray, exactly, but rather to tell God what a great guy he was. He could have at least given God credit for creating him that way. But his focus was on himself, not God. The tax collector was despised in the community. He took money from the Jews and gave it to the Romans. Nobody wanted to be his friend. He went to the temple because he recognized his sinfulness and knew what to do about it. He asked God for mercy. Jesus does not want us to be like the Pharisee—unaware that our problem is ourselves and our bloated egos. People around us will recognize our obvious pride, even if we don't. We are to be humble like the tax collector, taking our faulty selves before God's throne of grace and saying, "Please be merciful to me." God answers that prayer with a yes every time.

Whatever our problem, God's mercy is the answer.

COMMANDING GOD

Thus says the LORD, the Holy One of Israel, and his Maker:
"Ask Me of things to come concerning My sons;
and concerning the work of My hands, you command me."
ISAIAH 45:11 NKJV

After getting so close to the Christmas cake that he got icing on his nose,
a five-year-old boy was sternly told not to touch the delicious dessert.
To amuse himself, the boy decided to sing the birthday song to Jesus.
So he sang: "Happy birthday to You. Happy birthday to You.
Happy birthday, dear Jesus (don't touch the cake!).
Happy birthday to You."

We wouldn't dream of telling God what to do. Yet there were mighty men of God in the Old Testament who had the privilege of doing just that. Because they were living in the will of God, He allowed them to command Him. The Israelites were fighting the Amorites. The sun was going down, and Joshua realized that some of the Amorites would be able to escape in the darkness. Because God had told Joshua to destroy these people, Joshua said, "Sun, stand still" (Joshua 10:12 NKJV). And God made the sun stay in the sky until Joshua had destroyed the enemy. To bring Ahab's attention to the Lord, Elijah told him there would be a drought. And God shut up the heavens for three years. (See 1 Kings 17–18.) Amazing, that God would listen to His children and allow them the privilege of telling Him what to do.

We may not be able to tell God what to do,
but we can listen when He tells us what to do.

SUMMING IT UP

" 'You shall love the LORD your God with all your heart,
with all your soul, with all your strength, and with all your mind,'
and 'your neighbor as yourself.' "
LUKE 10:27 NKJV

A three-year-old boy's nanny overheard him say something mean to his
friend. Sitting the boy on the sofa, the nanny proceeded to give him a long
lecture on hospitality and friendship. When she had finished, she asked,
"Do you understand me?"
"Yes, ma'am," the boy replied.
"Then what did I just say?" she asked.
The boy replied, "Behave."

In the Old Testament, the Israelites were given the Ten
Commandments (see Exodus 20:2–17). In the New Testament,
those laws were summed up in just two commandments, as
expressed in Luke 10:27 above. When we love the Lord our
God with everything we have we won't have any other god
before Him or make graven images to worship or take His
name in vain or forget to honor His holy days. When we love
our neighbors as we love ourselves we will honor our parents;
we won't commit murder or adultery; we won't steal or bear false
witness or covet what our neighbor has. God's law has always
been summed up in one word—*love*. God is love, and He wants
us to love Him and each other. In Ephesians 6:12, Paul says that
we're not to be wrestling against flesh and blood—in other
words, we're not supposed to be fighting with each other. We're
to join together to build up and encourage one another.

When we obey God's commandments
we get along with each other and with Him.

TATTLING

A seven-year-old girl was given a lecture
about not tattling. Afterward, she ran into the room
where her mother and grandmother were talking
and announced breathlessly that her younger brother
was tattling in the other room.

As adults, we might think that we're too mature to tattle. But what about gossiping? Isn't that just another form of tattling? Some people think it's all right to repeat something if it is true. The Bible doesn't make that distinction. And neither should we. Whether a juicy tidbit is true or false, we are not to repeat it. Proverbs 6:16–19 gives a list of the things that God hates, the last one being "one who sows discord among brethren" (NKJV). Instead of tearing each other down, we are to edify and help each other, being careful of what we say, of the stories we tell. There was a minister who decided to preach a sermon called "The Evils of Gossip." Ironically, the hymn that was listed to be sung right after his message was "I Love to Tell the Story." What story are you telling? If we are busy telling people the good news that Jesus died to save us, we won't have time to spread the bad news about someone else.

We are to spread the Gospel, not gossip.

"The Bottom Line"

What does the LORD your God require of you, but to fear the LORD your God, to walk in all His ways and to love Him, to serve the LORD your God with all your heart and with all your soul, and to keep the commandments of the LORD and His statutes.
DEUTERONOMY 10:12–13 NKJV

*Taking a walk around the neighborhood with his nanny,
a three-year-old boy announced,
"If you go into a house with strangers, you get a spanking
and that's the bottom line!"*

Deuteronomy 10:12–13 states God's "bottom line" for us. We are to fear God and love Him. We show this by keeping all His commandments, which isn't as difficult as it sounds. When we love God with all our heart and soul, we find ourselves wanting not only to please Him but to show His love to others. A harsh man made a list of all the things he expected out of his wife in their marriage. The woman did her best to do everything on the list but it was hard because her husband was so demanding. A few years after they got married, the man died. The widow then married a man who was very different from her first husband. One day the woman came across the list her first husband had made for her. To her surprise she was doing everything on the list for her second husband. But now she found it easy because she did it out of love. So, too, our love for God makes following His commandments easy.

Loving God means doing what He requires of us.

FAITH

BEING OPTIMISTIC

Looking unto Jesus the author and finisher of our faith.
HEBREWS 12:2 KJV

A two-year-old girl was taken to visit the Infantry Museum.
One of the exhibits was a Bradley fighting vehicle.
The girl walked around the huge tank, bent down, looked underneath
it, then straightened up and kicked its treads. Turning to her father,
she held out her hand and said commandingly, "Keys."

Our worries may sometimes seem to us as big as a Bradley fighting vehicle. We lose heart when we look at the obstacles in our way instead of looking upward to God our salvation. Faith is not the absence of fear but trusting God *despite* it. Unforeseen situations and challenges come at us each moment, but God comes with them, too. We are to keep the faith no matter what happens, no matter how we feel or how dire our situation looks. In faith we turn over to God every battle that comes our way, every obstacle that blocks our path, and let Him handle it for us. In return, He strengthens our faith so that we can face anything. Faith also reminds us that God is in control, Master of the universe. We can rest easy because He's got a plan. Keep your eyes on God. He knows what He's doing.

Faith means we can relax because we know God is in control.

GOD IS ALWAYS RIGHT

As for God, His way is perfect; the word of the LORD is proven;
He is a shield to all who trust in Him.
2 SAMUEL 22:31 NKJV

"Sometimes," an eight-year-old child told her aunt,
"my mother is always right."

Feeling like we have to be right all the time can cause us great stress. But none of us can be right 100 percent of the time. Only God can. Since God's way is perfect, it makes good sense that we should follow His way—not ours. But to follow God, we have to have faith that He knows what He's doing. We have to believe that He's doing what's best for us. But how do we follow His way? By praying and by looking into His word—a lamp for our feet, a light on our path (see Psalm 119:105). His word gives us the faith to follow Him when we can only see one step at a time, even though we want to see the whole path ahead. God is our "cruise control," as well as our GPS. He keeps us at the right speed and on the right path. We don't have to worry about what lies around the bend. God already knows and He's got you covered. So go ahead. Move forward in faith and confidence. His light will illuminate your next step while His shield protects you.

Faith is believing that God will do what He said He will do.

"God Made Me This Way"

For we are His workmanship, created in Christ Jesus for good works,
which God prepared beforehand so that we would walk in them.
EPHESIANS 2:10 NASB

A mother asked her five-year-old daughter,
"How did you get to be so smart?"
The girl replied, "God made me this way."

God created each one of us to glorify Him in some way during our time upon this earth. And He made each of us unique. Even twins don't share the same fingerprint! In God's plan, there is something only *we* can do, and God created us to do that very thing. We are vital to His plan because He chose to work through us. As we look to God in faith, knowing that He has a specific plan for each of our lives, God enlarges our souls so that He can pour more of His love into us. Then we have more love to show and to serve others around us. God gives us the faith we need to follow Him wherever He leads us. As others see that faith, they'll want to know more about the God we serve. Are you allowing God to use you to do what only you can do or are you allowing the things of this world to deter you from fulfilling His plan?

God desires to work through you, not go around you.

"IF JESUS LOVES ME. . ."

But here is how God has shown his love for us.
While we were still sinners, Christ died for us.
ROMANS 5:8 NIrV

During children's church, a youth pastor was using candy hearts to
illustrate the love of Jesus. He gave each of the children a heart
and told them to give it to someone else. When the children gave away
their first heart, the pastor gave them each three more hearts.
The children quickly grasped the concept and kept giving away the
candy until the pastor ran out. To make his point, the pastor said,
"Unlike this candy, Jesus' love never runs out.
The more we share it, the more He gives us to share."
A six-year-old boy responded,
"If Jesus loves me, then why didn't I get any candy?"

Sometimes, while in the midst of a trial, such as a family crisis, financial trouble, or a serious illness, we may have a tendency to question God: If Jesus loves me, why [fill in the blank]?" But there is no "if." Jesus definitely loves us and He's proven it over and over. Our circumstances don't affect Jesus' love for us and shouldn't affect our love for Jesus. He knows what we're going through because He's going through it with us. In fact, we couldn't get through anything without the love of Jesus. We need not worry or wonder why. We only need to *know* that Jesus loves us. Amazing!

There is no greater love than the love of Jesus.

Trying to Understand

*A four-year-old woke her mother up at two in the morning and asked,
"Mommy, why do I have two eyeballs and only see one thing?"*

We want God to explain the unexplainable. But faith means leaning our entire human personality on God in absolute trust and confidence in His power, wisdom, and goodness. One reason God doesn't explain everything to us is because we would never be able to understand it. It would be like us trying to explain something to an ant. Another reason God doesn't make everything clear to us is because He doesn't have to. Faith in God means we are to trust Him to do whatever is right for us whether we understand it or not. It can be frustrating for us when we try to explain something to our children and they just don't get it. One mother was frantic because she couldn't get her three-year-old son to understand that he couldn't play in the busy street. Although he cried and wanted to go outside, she couldn't let him because even when she was with him, he ran straight into the street. In the same way, we sometimes don't understand that what we want to do will actually hurt us. God knows and He protects us from ourselves. Just trust Him.

Even with two eyes, we should only see the Lord.

"We're going N!"

*By faith Abraham obeyed when he was called to go out
to the place which he would receive as an inheritance.
And he went out, not knowing where he was going.*
HEBREWS 11:8 NKJV

*A four-year-old boy was fascinated by the digital compass on the
mirror of his mother's car. "What is that?" he asked her.
His mother replied, "It tells us what direction we are going in."
A little later the boy said excitedly, "We're going N! We're going N!"*

Life can be very complicated. We may not have a clear idea of
where we're headed and that can be scary. If we were Abraham,
we probably would have asked for a map before we left Ur.
But God gave us Abraham as an example of how He leads
us. Abraham didn't ask for a map; he just followed God. We
don't *need* a map, really; we just *want* one. But God wants us to
follow Him because we trust Him to know where we are going.
Our circumstances will be exactly the same whether we have
faith or not. What faith does is change us and how we meet
the challenges God gives us. We may not know what direction
our paths will take on this earth, but we do know our ultimate
destination—God has promised us eternal life with Him. Our
faith in that promise will make following His path for us easier.

**Let us be like Abraham, with unwavering faith and belief
that God has the power to do what He has promised.**

Wishing

*Faith is being sure of what we hope for.
It is being certain of what we do not see.*
HEBREWS 11:1 NIrV

*A five-year-old was told to make a wish,
and then throw her penny into the fountain.
"What did you wish for?" her mother asked her.
"That my penny would hit the water," the girl replied.*

Jesus said, "Ask, and it will be given to you" (Luke 11:9 NIrV). But He didn't say what would be given. He said, "Everyone who asks will receive" (Luke 11:10 NIrV). But what will we receive? Whatever is best for us. It might not be what we *think* is best, but it is what our Father *knows* is best for us. We don't always know what we want or what we should wish for, but God does—for He is all seeing and all knowing. Whatever we hope for, He knows and gives us what is best for us. All we need to do is pray, "Thy will be done." In faith, we can focus on God instead of our circumstances. We can repeat to ourselves, "I'll let God handle this. He knows what He's doing and He's never let me down." God will answer our prayers beyond what we could ever expect or imagine.

God gives His best to those who leave the choice with Him.

OVERCOMING

A five-year-old boy was watching the film King Kong.
At the end of the movie, a bystander says to King Kong's handler,
"Those planes really took care of King Kong, didn't they?"
King Kong's handler replies, "It wasn't the planes.
It was beauty that killed the beast."
At that point, the boy said to his father, "No. It was the planes!"

There is so much evil in this world. It could be easy to get overwhelmed by it, as evil, at times, seems as big as King Kong. But the planes of our faith can overcome evil. One woman would get what she called "The Nameless Dreads." During those times she would feel awful, as if something bad was going to happen even though she didn't know specifically what. Some days she wouldn't even get out of bed because the dread was so overwhelming. But then she learned to focus on God and not the ominous feeling. She used her faith to overcome "The Nameless Dreads" by realizing that no matter what came along, God was with her and would make it right. No matter how much evil there is, God is bigger and the faith He gives us is strong enough to overcome it.

We do not let evil overcome us. We overcome evil with our faith.

DOING OUR PART

*Do you see that faith was working together with his works,
and by works faith was made perfect?*
JAMES 2:22 NKJV

*During a church service, a fifth-grade boy whispered to his mother,
"Please tell the preacher not to talk so loud. He's keeping me awake."*

God is faithful to us and He expects us to be faithful to Him. One of the ways we show our fidelity is by our service to or for others. As God's representatives here on earth, our faith comes with social obligations. We are to bless those around us so they will see our good works, which will hopefully point them to our Father. Pray that God will open your eyes to the needs of those around you and give you the wisdom you need to help others in any way you can. Each step of faith you take—in or out of your comfort zone—will bring you closer to God. Another way we show our fidelity is by assembling with fellow Christians. People who are not believers monitor our church attendance to see if we are practicing what we preach. They want to see if we believe in God enough to worship Him every Sunday. And our fellow believers also monitor our attendance at church where, hopefully, the preacher is keeping us awake.

God is faithfulness personified, and we are the image of God.

THE FAMILY OF GOD

"For whoever does the will of My Father who is in heaven,
he is My brother and sister and mother."
MATTHEW 12:50 NASB

During a Sunday school lesson, a teacher told
her class that "John the Baptist was a cousin to Jesus."
One of the children raised his hand.
"Teacher," he said, "did Jesus have any Methodist relatives?"

There is an old poem:

To live above with saints of old—oh, won't that be glory!
To live below with saints we know, well, that's a different story.

Jesus has relatives in every denomination because every one of us who obeys God is related to Jesus. That means we are one big, happy family. Sometimes our faith is tested by the way other members of our family are behaving. But we are not to focus on them; we are to focus on the Father of us all.

The only place to shelter is beneath God's wings.
He takes the stones that hurtful people sling
At us and changes them, by His mighty power
Into His peace which our faith lets flower.

God brings people into our lives so that we can learn how to get along with them. And although we can't control what other people do, we can control our own thoughts and reactions by giving God full rein of our minds and hearts.

We are all the children of God,
and it is His place to correct others, not ours.

"A Bad Word"

[Jesus said,] "For every idle word men may speak, they will give account of it in the day of judgment."
MATTHEW 12:36 NKJV

A family was watching the movie Home Alone.
As Macaulay Culkin's young character ran from the burglars,
he said a bad word. The five-year-old son of the family watching
the film looked at his mother to see her reaction. She said,
"He said a bad word, didn't he?"
The son replied, "But it's probably okay,
because his parents are on a plane to Paris."

Sometimes we think we can get away with saying a swear word—that maybe God isn't listening to us at that precise moment. But the Bible says that every word we say is broadcast in heaven. Realizing that might make us a little more careful when we speak. Jesus also said that whatever comes out of our mouths, comes out of our hearts (see Matthew 12:35). Do we have a heart full of swear words? If so, with what are we filling it? If a cup is full and we accidentally knock it over, whatever was in the cup spills everywhere. When life knocks us over, what comes out of us? No matter what our circumstances, let's strive not to utter profanities but praises to God.

God hears everything we say—the good, the bad, and the ugly.

"DIDN'T SIN ALL THAT MUCH"

Everyone has sinned. No one measures up to God's glory.
ROMANS 3:23 NIrV

To make a point about sin, a Sunday school teacher said to her class of
fourth graders, "But, of course, you are all too young to sin."
"We've sinned," some of the children in the class assured her.
"We've lied and cheated and disobeyed."
"And that's why Jesus died," the teacher told them, "for your sins."
"Well," said one student, "we didn't sin all that much."

Fortunately for us, God didn't stop with the verse above. If He had, we'd be lost. But Romans 6:23 tells us that God gave us an incredible gift—eternal life through Jesus. Because God loves us, He extends to us His wonderful, awesome, amazing *grace*, defined as God's undeserved favor. We cannot earn grace. It is a gift from God that saves us all from sin, even if we think we haven't sinned all that much. It is because of His grace that God is so willing to forgive us no matter how many times we miss the mark. We can never comprehend the fullness of God's love for us and His grace extended to us. All we can do is stand in awe of our wonderful, powerful God and thank Him for His indescribable gifts of love, grace, and mercy.

Because of God's grace, we are saved. Thank God!

"I BETTER WILL"

"Watch and pray, lest you enter into temptation.
The spirit indeed is willing, but the flesh is weak."
MATTHEW 26:41 NKJV

A two-year-old girl was fascinated with her new baby sister.
For some reason, she kept trying to poke the baby in the eye,
an act for which the girl's mother scolded the two-year-old several times.
The mother, keeping a close watch, again saw the two-year-old walking
toward the baby's crib with her little finger pointed, ready to poke.
"You'd better not," the mother said.
"I better will," replied the two-year-old and kept walking.

Sometimes we can't resist ourselves. Instead of watching and praying to be kept from temptation, we are right there eyeballing it. Where was Eve when she was tempted? Hanging out in the middle of the Garden of Eden, looking at the forbidden tree. The old saying, "Idle hands are the devil's workshop," rings of truth. Banality breeds bad behavior. But when we are actively doing our part to further the Kingdom of God, we don't have the time to be tempted into sinning. So stay active for God. And in those downtimes, instead of asserting your will by telling God, "I better will," acknowledge that God's will is better, and then follow His plans for your life. Having trouble resisting? Pray for God's help and power. Then get busy serving Him.

Watching and praying gives us the
spiritual strength to fight temptation.

Keeping It Simple

Let this mind be in you, which was also in Christ Jesus.
PHILIPPIANS 2:5 KJV

A ten-year-old girl came home from camp
and proudly handed her mother a "scroll"
she had made. On it, she had printed the Lord's Prayer.
Examining what her daughter had written,
the mother smiled to herself when she read,
"Forgive us our depths."

Because of the Ten Commandments, in days past, Christianity was often referred to as the religion of the "shalt nots." Basically it was thought that Christianity was a dreary, joyless religion bounded by rules that forbade anything even remotely considered to be fun. Nothing could be further from the truth. Christians are followers of Christ. And Jesus was a joyful person. The verse above sums up Christianity quite well. We simply look at Christ and have the same mindset He had. We don't need formality and rules and procedures. We don't need "depths." We just need Jesus. We follow Jesus like Jesus followed His Father. Every day we ask our Father what His will is for us and then we do that. Simple. Humans have a tendency to want to complicate things. But God's will is simple—let the mind of Jesus Christ be in you.

When we have the mind of Christ,
we stay closer to the heart of our Father.

"Kinky Turtles"

*Lift up your heads, O you gates; yes, lift them up, you age-abiding
doors, that the King of glory may come in. Who is [He then] this King
of glory? The Lord of hosts, He is the King of glory.
Selah [pause, and think of that]!*
Psalm 24:9–10 AMP

*One Sunday morning a four-year-old preacher's son asked his father,
"Are the kinky turtles coming to church today?"
Completely baffled, the father said, "What kinky turtles?"
"We sang their song last week," his son explained.
"'Lead On, Oh Kinky Turtles' ['Lead On, O King Eternal']."*

God isn't kinky. But He is the King of kings and Lord of lords.
It is truly amazing grace that this awesome, wonderful being
who is all powerful, all knowing, and everywhere present should
take notice of us. And even more amazing is that God doesn't
condescend to us. He doesn't treat us like slaves, as if He is
superior and we are inferior—which we are. He treats us like
His beloved children whom He adores. The Bible says we are
the apple of God's eye (see Deuteronomy 32:10; Zechariah 2:8).
And no matter what we do, we cannot exhaust the grace of God.
Imagine God's grace is a huge mountain of sand, and we are
trying to remove it one grain at a time. It can't be done. When
was the last time we put the *amazing* back into God's amazing
grace?

**"Amazing Grace" isn't just a song;
it is the foundation of our salvation.**

Learning the Hard Stuff

"Come to Me, all you who labor and are heavy laden, and I will give you rest. . . . For My yoke is easy and My burden is light."
MATTHEW 11:28, 30 NKJV

*A four-year-old girl came home from school and announced
that she could write her name. "That's great," said her grandmother.
"Will you write your name for me?"
"Okay," the girl replied, "but I'll need help with the hard part."
"What's the hard part?" her grandmother asked.
"Writing my name," said the girl.*

We, too, need help with the hard stuff. Life can be extremely difficult at times. Here's the good news: Jesus not only will tell us what to do, He will do it through us and with us. He tells us that His yoke is easy. When two animals were yoked together, they could pull simultaneously and lessen the burden on each other. When we're yoked to Jesus He takes the entire burden upon Himself. When we walk with Him He carries our entire load for us. What a wonderful Savior! He works His will through us and then tells us, "Well done, good and faithful servant" (Matthew 25:23 NKJV). He does all the work and then gives us the credit. All the hard stuff becomes easier because we have Jesus to help us.

Nothing is too hard to bear when we yoke ourselves to Jesus.

"Pray for Me"

*No temptation has overtaken you except such as is common to man;
but God is faithful, who will not allow you to be tempted beyond
what you are able, but with the temptation
will also make the way of escape.*

1 Corinthians 10:13 NKJV

*A four-year-old boy was misbehaving in church.
His mother shushed him several times and, when he continued to act
up, took him by the hand and began to lead him out of the sanctuary.
As they made their way toward the door,
the boy stopped and called out,
"Y'all, pray for me."*

That's what we all want—mercy. We would like very much to
escape the consequences of what we've done. *Mercy* means we
don't get what we deserve. *Grace* means we get what we don't
deserve. God's mercy and grace go hand in hand with His love
for us. With every temptation that comes our way, God provides
a way for us to avoid yielding to that temptation. Many times,
when we ignore God's escape route and deliberately choose to
give in to temptation, God still shields us from the consequences
of our actions. That's grace. That's mercy. That's amazing. Where
would we be without the grace and mercy of God?

*Our merciful God, full of grace, provides us
with a means of escape. We need only seek it.*

Prejudiced

*Do not hold the faith of our Lord Jesus Christ,
the Lord of glory, with partiality.*
JAMES 2:1 NKJV

*On the way to church one Sunday morning,
a ten-year-old boy asked his aunt if she was prejudiced.
Shocked, his aunt said, "Why would you ask me that?"
"Well," said the ten-year-old,
"I just wanted to know if you were prejudiced
or Methodist or what religion you are."*

God extends His grace to all. We can do no less. In fact, we have no right to try to withhold His grace from anyone—rich or poor, black or white, male or female, slave or free. Unfortunately there is prejudice in this world. But we are not of this world. We are just pilgrims here waiting to go to our real home in heaven. As we pass through this world, one of our purposes is to spread the message of the love and grace of God. And, as James said in the verse above, we are to do so without partiality. We don't get to pick and choose who should be allowed to hear God's message. The Bible says Jesus died for all. *All* means all. God's grace is extended to everyone, "for God does not show favoritism" (Romans 2:11 NIV). He allows His good blessings to fall on the just and the unjust (see Matthew 5:44–45). Got God's grace? Extend it to everyone the same way He does—without prejudice.

Since God extends His grace to all, we can do no less.

"TOOK AN ATTITUDE"

*Let your speech at all times be gracious (pleasant and winsome),
seasoned [as it were] with salt,
[so that you may never be at a loss]
to know how you ought to answer anyone
[who puts a question to you].*
COLOSSIANS 4:6 AMP

*A mother was astonished to receive a call from her four-year-old
daughter's preschool teacher who told her the girl
had hit a little boy in class.
The mother was amazed because her daughter was not aggressive at all.
When she got her daughter home, the mother said to her,
"Why did you hit Billy?" The girl put her little hands on her hips
and said, "He took an attitude with me."*

Most of us know people who have taken an attitude with us. The question is: What attitude do we take with them? The more important question is: What attitude do we take with God? Because God is gracious to us, even when we're "naughty," we're on God's "nice" list. In fact, our salvation comes as an expression of that grace. But we don't want to take advantage of God's grace. We want to be grateful for it. Our attitude toward God should be gratitude. And our attitude toward others should be an extension of God's redeeming grace. Thus we must watch how we use our hands (actions) and our mouths (speech), making sure they are filled with grace.

**Because of God's glorious grace,
we can always have a generous and pleasing attitude.**

Forgetting

"For I will forgive their iniquity,
and their sin I will remember no more."
JEREMIAH 31:34 NKJV

A nine-year-old boy told his grandfather,
"I remember everything except what I forget."

Isn't that true of all of us? We remember everything except what we forget. Only God has the ability to forget things willfully. And what does He choose to forget? Our sins. How wonderful. Some people have the idea that when Judgment Day comes, all our past sins will be paraded before us and we will be called on to account for them. Not so. Jesus already paid for every sin we could ever commit—past, present, and future. For Christians, Judgment Day is reward day. Matthew 25:31–46 says that believers are Jesus' sheep. He calls us the beloved of His Father and tells us that we are inheriting His kingdom. For the goats, however, Judgment Day is going to be rough. Their sins will not be forgotten. Why? Because they refused to allow God to graciously forgive them. They refused to accept Jesus' wondrous sacrifice and atoning work. God will remember their sins and they will be sorry for them then, but it will be too late. But it is not too late for us to tell them the good news—Jesus died so that God could forgive and forget our sins.

Many people in this world are in
desperate need of God's gracious salvation.
It's up to us to spread the Word.

The Image of God

Then God said, "Let us make man in our likeness."
GENESIS 1:26 NIrV

A mother teasingly called her four-year-old daughter "monkey butt."
To her surprise, her daughter immediately got upset.
"Don't call me that," the girl said. "Monkeys are ugly."
"I'm sorry," the mother apologized.
"What would you like me to call you?"
"Princess butt," her daughter replied.

In the beginning, God made Adam and Eve in His own perfect likeness—and all was well with the world. But then Adam and Eve sinned and lost the likeness of God. Adam then "became the father of a son in his own likeness, according to his image" (Genesis 5:3 NASB). So, how do we, descendants of this imperfect, sinful couple, get back to being God's image? By becoming like Christ. For when Jesus Christ died for our sins and rose again, our ability to be the image of God was restored to us. By His grace, God is daily transforming us into the likeness of Jesus. As we put on Christ and grow daily in His grace and wisdom, others can more clearly see what the image of God should look like. We are new creatures— reborn in the light of Christ! Showing His shining image to the world around us is an awesome responsibility because the world looks at us in order to see God. Imagine that!

We are the image of God once again.

GROWING IN CHRIST

*For whatsoever things were written aforetime
were written for our learning, that we through patience
and comfort of the scriptures might have hope.*
ROMANS 15:4 KJV

*A five-year-old boy insisted that his mother
watch him come down the stairs
on his birthday so that she could see how much bigger he was.*

Our children are proud of growing up. They want us to measure how tall they are and count how old they are. We who are physically grown want to grow spiritually in Christ. We want to be more mature. But sometimes we might feel like we are stagnating. Looking at how farmers use their land can teach us a valuable lesson. Every so often, a farmer will let a field lie fallow for a year. Nothing is planted in it. It is allowed to rest. Nature comes and reclaims some of the field. Then the next year, when the field is tilled, fertilized, and seeded, the plants grow stronger and better because the field was allowed to rest. Sometimes God wants us to be fallow fields, to rest so that we can renew our energies and our strength. We may think that we are being shunted to the side, but that is not the case at all. God told the Israelites that every seventh year they were to allow their fields to rest (see Leviticus 25:1–7). We are more important to God than fields. Once we have rested, we are ready to begin to grow again. And the seeds planted in us will bear more fruit.

**Being fallow doesn't mean we're done.
It just means that we are taking a much needed rest.**

FEBRUARY OUT

*So teach us to number our days,
that we may get us a heart of wisdom.*
PSALM 90:12 AMP

*An eight-year-old girl told her mother,
"I looked at the calendar and February is all out."*

Time is running out and that is a good thing for us because one day time will be no more and we'll be with our Father. What a glorious hope we have looking forward to that day. In the meantime, we need to use wisely the time we do have by getting to know God and the power of His love for us. While we wait for His glorious appearing, we endeavor to learn what His purpose is for us as individuals. We follow His commands to teach our children about Him, to be His witnesses, to love our neighbors, and to love Him with all our hearts and souls and minds. We use the time to walk "worthy of the Lord unto all pleasing, being fruitful in every good work, and increasing in the knowledge of God" (Colossians 1:10 KJV). This is God's will and plan for us. We live our lives in the expectation of Jesus' return. This hope makes life on this earth not just merely existing but joyfully living. What a wonderful Savior we have. " 'Surely I am coming quickly.' Amen. Even so, come, Lord Jesus!" (Revelation 22:20 NKJV).

Jesus gives us great expectations!

FOLDED CLOTHES

*And set your minds and keep them set on what is above
(the higher things), not on the things that are on the earth.*
COLOSSIANS 3:2 AMP

*A seven-year-old girl was watching
a video about the resurrection of Christ.
When the empty tomb was shown, she said,
"Oh, look. He folded His clothes so neatly."*

Sometimes it's easy to overlook the familiar and get distracted by irrelevant details. But we want to keep our minds set on spiritual aspects. Whatever situation we are in or are going through, God has a spiritual lesson for us to learn. Is someone being unkind to us? Saul was very unkind to David, but David saw Saul as God's tool to help David grow spiritually (see 1 Samuel 24:16–22). Have we lost all that we hold dear? Job said, "The LORD gave, and the LORD has taken away; blessed be the name of the LORD" (Job 1:21 NKJV). Are we looking into Jesus' empty tomb? Then we surely see the greatest love ever shown being freely given to us (see John 15:13). When we focus on Jesus and His love for us, we suddenly find that whatever we're going through is bearable because Jesus has given us hope and our hope gives us faith and our faith gives us the ability to trust Him completely. So we don't see folded clothes; we see life everlasting.

**When we keep our focus on the Lord,
we see opportunities, not obstacles.**

"Happy News"

And the Lord blessed the latter days of Job more than his beginning.
JOB 42:12 AMP

A woman was having a difficult day. Her refrigerator was leaking water all over the kitchen floor. Her sister had called to say she was ill and needed some help. Her dog got loose from the yard and she had to chase him all over the neighborhood.
When the phone rang, she said, "This had better not be any more bad news. I need some happy news."
Her ten-year-old grandson said, "I'm smart, Gran."

We all need happy news and we can have it—Christ in you, the hope of glory. No matter what goes wrong, we have our sights on things above and know that, for us, this world is the worst that it gets. All our good news is yet to come and, like Job, our latter days will be so much more blessed than our beginnings. How do we know this? Because Ephesians 1:14 says the Holy Spirit is our "earnest" (KJV). In the days during which the King James Bible was written, the word *earnest* referred to the token one gave to his betrothed as a pledge of his love. Today, it would be an engagement ring. We are the Bride of Christ and the Holy Spirit has been given to us as a pledge of Jesus' love for us. Happy news indeed! And God wants us to share our happy news with others, to give them the same hope we have—the hope of glory.

Jesus gives us hope so that we can share that hope with others.

"Harvest Vegetable"

*"Blessed are those who are called
to the marriage supper of the Lamb!"*
REVELATION 19:9 NKJV

*A five-year-old girl announced that she was going to a vegetable.
"A vegetable?" her mother asked.
"Yes," said the girl.
"Friday is our Harvest Vegetable [Festival] at school."*

One day we will attend the festival to end all festivals. We have been invited to the marriage supper of the Lamb. And we're not just invited—we're the Bride! Lots of women have spent many wonderful hours planning their weddings. Everything has to be just so. There are lists and more lists and all sorts of details to be decided on. Now imagine that God has planned the wedding. It boggles our minds. We cannot possibly imagine all the wonderful things God has planned for the marriage of His Son to His Bride, the church. It is a mystery how we can be so many individuals and still be only one Bride—but it's true! Some consider the Song of Solomon to be an allegory of the love between Jesus and the church. The book describes how we look to Him and how much He loves us. It is all mysterious to us now, but what a day that will be! What a joyful time we have to look forward to. We are truly blessed!

*The marriage of the Lamb won't be the wedding of the century;
it will be the wedding of eternity.*

Jesus Said, "Ha. Ha."

*Thanks be to God! He gives us the victory
through our Lord Jesus Christ.*
1 Corinthians 15:57 NIV

*For an Easter project, a ten-year-old boy drew a picture
showing the empty tomb with the stone rolled away.
Underneath he wrote, "Jesus said, 'Ha. Ha.'"*

Sometimes our children can express the most profound spiritual truths in the simplest terms. That is one of the reasons Jesus said that to enter the Kingdom, we must have the faith of a child. This boy understood on the deepest level what Jesus did for us—He conquered sin and death. What a miracle! We never could have done it. We aren't qualified. But God loves us so much that He wants to save us from our sins and follies. He doesn't want any of us to perish. And so Jesus came to love us, die for us, and save us. To a world hopelessly lost in sin, Jesus brought hope. God gives us so many things—love, joy, peace, mercy, and hope. He cares about our human condition and offers us comfort that this world is not our home. We have the hope of a bright and glorious future with our King of kings and Lord of lords. Blessed be the name of the Lord!

Paul's hope was that he might know Christ and the power of His resurrection (see Philippians 3:10). May that be our hope also.

GOD HAS OUR NUMBER

"But the very hairs of your head are all numbered. Do not fear therefore; you are of more value than many sparrows."
LUKE 12:7 NKJV

A woman answered her phone and heard a little voice say,
"Is John there?" "I'm sorry," the woman said gently,
"you have the wrong number." "Oh," said the little voice.
"Well, do you know John's number?"

God knows all about us, even down to the number of hairs on our heads. He knows why He created us and what He created us to do. We don't want to get sidetracked from our purpose here. When Ezra brought his group from Babylon back to Jerusalem, he did the job God put him there to do. He became a scribe. He worked with Nehemiah to ensure the rebuilding of Jerusalem, the city walls, and the temple. Ezra was descended from the line of Aaron (Ezra 7:2–7)—and he may have wanted to be a priest. But Ezra didn't go around worrying about why he wasn't a priest; he kept focused on what God wanted him to do. We don't need to spend our time looking for validation of who we are and why we're here. God knows why He created us, and He knows what He created us to do. God has already validated us. And there is no greater validation than that.

Actively doing what God put us here to do
will keep us from getting sidetracked.

More

*A two-year-old girl carried her piggy bank around
with her and was pleased when adults put money in it.
"What do you say?" her mother prompted her.
The girl held out her bank and said, "More."*

When Solomon became king, he was afraid. He felt that he was too young to rule and that maybe no one would respect him. The Lord appeared to Solomon in a dream and asked him what he wanted. Solomon asked God for an understanding heart so that he could judge God's people correctly. God was so pleased with Solomon's answer that He granted his request. Then He added, "I have also given you what you have not asked: both riches and honor, so that there shall not be anyone like you among the kings all your days" (1 Kings 3:13 NKJV). Solomon only asked for understanding. God gave him that and so much more. Famous for his wisdom and his wealth, Solomon's reputation spread all over the world, prompting the queen of Sheba to check it out for herself. After visiting with Solomon, the queen left, saying, "The report I heard doesn't even begin to tell the whole story about you" (1 Kings 10:7 NIrv). That's the way it is with all of God's blessings—the whole has not been told to us.

**With God there is always more.
He blesses us and blesses us again.**

Treasures in Heaven

"Eye has not seen, nor ear heard, nor have entered into the heart of man the things which God has prepared for those who love Him."
1 CORINTHIANS 2:9 NKJV

A four-year-old girl asked her mother, "
Mom, when you go 'up there'
do you get to take all your stuff?"
Her mother replied, "Up where?"
"Up in heaven," said the girl.
"Do you get to take all your stuff with you?"
Her mother said, "No, sweetheart, you don't take anything with you
when you go to heaven."
"But, Mom," protested the daughter,
"I want to take my Hello Kitty underwear when I go."

We may smile at what our children consider precious. To us adults, a child's treasures may seem quite silly. But what about our treasures? Jesus told us to lay up our treasures in heaven for where our treasures are there will our hearts be (see Matthew 6:20–21). So what do we really deem as precious? Our children? It is an awesome responsibility to know that our influence will affect our children all their lives. We need to be sure that we are laying a good foundation for them so that our most precious treasures—these children the Lord has blessed us with—will be "laid up" in heaven.

We have no real idea of what God
has in store for us and our children,
but we do know that it is spectacular beyond all imaginings.

Anticipation

*"There has not failed one word of His good promise,
which He promised through His servant Moses."*
1 KINGS 8:56 NKJV

*An eight-year-old girl came home from school all excited
because her class was going to see a movie the next day.
It was all she could talk about that evening until her parents had
enough and sent her off to bed. The next morning, she got up,
still excited. She couldn't wait to get to school.
When the girl got home that afternoon, her mother said,
"So how was your day?"
"Pretty good," the girl replied,
"except we had to sit through this long, boring movie."*

Sometimes an eagerly anticipated event disappoints us when it finally arrives. That never happens with God. We can look forward to the fulfillment of His promises because it will be even more than we can imagine. In Revelation 2 and 3, there are many rewards promised to those who overcome: They will eat from the tree of life. They won't be hurt by the second death. They will be given hidden manna to eat. They will receive a new name known only to God. They will have power over the nations. They will be clothed in white garments. Jesus will confess their names before His Father. They will not be blotted out of the Book of Life. They will be made a pillar in the temple of God. Jesus will write on them His new name. There are even more promises than these. What wonders we have to look forward to.

**We look forward with great anticipation
to the realization of heaven.**

INFLUENCE

CHURCH WITH JESUS

Some of the Pharisees in the crowd said to Jesus,
"Teacher, rebuke your disciples!" "I tell you,"
he replied, "if they keep quiet, the stones will cry out."
LUKE 19:39–40 NIV

As a family was going into church,
the mother pointed out the Nativity scene
to her four-year-old son. "There's the Baby Jesus," she said.
With awe in his voice, her son said, "I go to church with Baby Jesus."

Are we, like this four-year-old boy, filled with awe because we go to church with Jesus? Jesus told the Pharisees that if His disciples didn't praise Him, the stones would. Perhaps we need to be a little more enthusiastic with our praises in church.

Oh, I cannot keep silent—
A song burst forth from me—
A song of praise to God above
Whom all around I see.
I sing His love and daily care;
The Christ of Calvary;
I sing of blessings from on high
And all He's done for me.

Every time we are in church, we celebrate being a part of God's universal family and that we are committed to one another and to God. As we rejoice in going to church with Jesus, the community around us will feel His presence among us. Like the psalmist, let's "Shout for joy to the LORD" (Psalm 100:1 NIV)!

We can't let stones do our job of praising Jesus.

"ONE. . .TWO. . .THREE. . ."

"Not my will, but yours be done."
LUKE 22:42 NIV

A mother, trying to get her two-and-a-half-year old daughter
to behave, tried the disciplinary method of counting to three.
It seemed to work well.
One day the little girl told her mother that she wanted a bath.
Her mother was busy and said, "Give me a minute, honey."
The little girl replied, "Mommy, I want a bath. One. . .two. . .three."

Obviously this child thought that counting to three was a magic formula to get her mother to do what she wanted her to do. Some people think of prayer that way. But prayer is not giving orders; it's reporting for duty. It is not a way for us to control God, but to give Him control over us. Jesus gave us the "magic formula" for prayer—"Not my will, but yours be done." Our prayers are influenced by what we believe. If we believe that we can nag God into giving us what we want then we will pray that way. If we believe that we need something right this minute then we will pray impatiently. But if we believe, truly believe, that God knows best, we will pray humbly and patiently for His will to be done on earth as it is in heaven (see Matthew 6:10). In doing so, we open up our hearts, minds, and souls to Him who always ends up giving us more than we can ever ask or imagine.

May the will of God surround us until
we see that His way is the only way to go.

Being Polite

If it is possible, as much as depends on you,
live peaceably with all men.
ROMANS 12:18 NKJV

A five-year-old boy had just had his first ride on a horse.
As the youngster started to walk away, the horse snorted.
Turning back, the boy said, "Bless you."

God expects us to go beyond just being polite when dealing with others. Having good manners is not enough. God has clear guidelines on how He wants us to interact:

> "Love one another" (John 13:34–35 NKJV).
> Do not backbite nor do evil to your neighbor (see Psalm 15:3).
> Teach younger Christians how to be mature (see Titus 2:4–8)
>   in both word and deed (see 1 Timothy 4:12).
> "Bear one another's burdens" (Galatians 6:2 NKJV).
> Be kind and forgiving (see Ephesians 4:32).
> "Encourage one another" (1 Thessalonians 5:11 NIV).

This is by no means a complete list, but it gives us the basics on interpersonal relationships. Sharing God's love in word and deed, instructing them spiritually, bearing the weight of problems, forgiving, being forgiven, and cheering others on reminds us how much and how often God does those things for us. It's a win-win! But sometimes, although we are doing everything we can to live peaceably with someone, it isn't possible—not because we aren't trying to get along with him or her but because the other person refuses to cooperate. As long as we do what we can, we can leave the results to God.

It takes more than just politeness to live peaceably with others.

BOOKS OF THE BIBLE

Your word is a lamp to my feet and a light to my path.
PSALM 119:105 NKJV

After playing Bible games for several weeks in Sunday school class,
an eight-year-old girl complained to her mother,
"I learned all the books of the Bible and I didn't even mean to."

Compare this child's attitude with children at another church where they were promised a Bible if they would learn the books of the Bible and recite them in front of the congregation. They eagerly took on this task. After a month, they were ready. One by one they recited, then received their Bibles. Two months later, not one of them remembered what they had learned. In yet another church, a group of teenagers told their new Sunday school teacher they had never learned the books of the Bible, even though most of them had been going to that church their whole lives. "And you can't make us learn them" was their general attitude. All these children are illustrations of the seeds within the parable of the sower (see Matthew 13:3–23). The eight-year-old would be the seed that was choked by thorns. The eager group of children would be the seeds that sprouted instantly on stony ground but died because they had no depth. The teenagers would be those seeds that fell by the wayside. None of these children were the seeds that fell on good ground—that would be the Bereans who searched the scriptures diligently to see if what Paul preached to them was true or not.

Learning the books of the Bible is good
but learning what's in them is better.

Counting Our Blessings

Blessed be the God and Father of our Lord Jesus Christ,
who has blessed us with every spiritual blessing
in the heavenly places in Christ.
EPHESIANS 1:3 NKJV

Having watched Disney's Toy Story, a four-year-old boy
constantly demanded a "Woody pocket."
Finally, his mother figured out that he meant a holster.

Our children want things. They want toys other children have. They want cereals they see advertised on TV. They just want. Sometimes this attitude overcomes us adults. We see things and we just want. But because we are not children, we know the antidote to this "wanton" attitude: gratitude. Instead of looking at things we don't have, we look at all the riches God has blessed us with, which makes us even more aware of all the things He has given us. And, when we share those blessings, we bless others, as well as ourselves, rejoicing in God's goodness. Praise flows naturally from a thankful heart, one that knows we don't really need any more to be thankful for. Jesus died for our sins and rose again to give us everlasting life in Him. He is all we ever needed or ever will need. Counting our blessings and sharing them with others shows our children that we have an attitude of gratitude and teaches them to share with others. And when we count our blessings, we count our children among them.

God has blessed us "to infinity and beyond"!

Discovering Ourselves

*Yet amid all these things we are more than conquerors and gain
a surpassing victory through Him Who loved us.*
ROMANS 8:37 AMP

*A three–year-old girl watched Disney's Hercules movie so often
that she could and did quote the dialogue along with it, word for word.
At one point in the movie, Hermes says, "I haven't seen this much love
in a room since Narcissus discovered himself."
The three-year-old said, "I haven't seen this much love
in a room since Sis Sis uncovered himself."*

As we journey through life, we all spend time trying to discover who we really are and why we are here on this earth. Although we haven't arrived yet, we discover that our journey is, at times, fascinating, joyful, and exciting. And when the road gets rough and somewhat perilous, we are assured that we are not walking alone. God is holding our hand, counseling and guiding us, loving us (see Psalm 73:23). Even more amazing is that He already knows who we are, where we're going, and what we're going to do. He knows all our inner and outer dialogue: "Before a word is on my tongue you, LORD, know it completely" (Psalm 139:4 NIV). We also travel this road with fellow believers, our loving companions along the Way. As we share our journey together, we walk side by side, comparing the maps that God has helped us make as we travel along. What precious love and companionship we encounter on this life journey!

**God knew us and loved us before we were even born
(see Psalm 139:15).**

"He's Hot!"

"Do not look at his appearance or at his physical stature, because I have refused him. For the LORD does not see as man sees; for man looks at the outward appearance, but the LORD looks at the heart."
1 SAMUEL 16:7 NKJV

A grandmother was driving down the road
when suddenly her nine-year-old granddaughter cried, "Nana, look!"
Startled, the grandmother said, "Don't yell at me when I'm driving."
"But, Nana," her granddaughter said,
"you have to look at that boy in the car next to us. He's hot!"

Some of us, despite everything we know to the contrary, still have a tendency to judge people by their appearance. We may instantly be attracted to a good-looking person or be put off by a not so good-looking one. But, as the saying goes, you can't judge a book (people) by its cover (their looks). In reality, we don't have much to do with the way we look. Oh, with makeup, hairdos, and clothes, we can make the best of what we have, but our general looks are beyond our control because that's the way God made us. When Samuel came to anoint a new king from among Jesse's sons, Samuel was surprised that the Lord didn't pick the oldest, Eliab. In Samuel's eye, Eliab seemed to have a lot going for him. But God said, "Don't judge by appearance." That still holds true for us today, too.

It takes awhile to learn about other people,
but it is worth the effort.

"Hide and Sneak"

"No one can serve two masters. Either you will hate the one and love the other, or you will be devoted to the one and despise the other. You cannot serve both God and money."
LUKE 16:13 NIV

A four-year-old boy said to his brother, "Let's play hide and sneak."

No one likes a sneak, especially when it comes to doing business. We want everyone we deal with to be honest and true. One woman said that being a Christian had nothing to do with her business. She thought it was perfectly all right to cheat people as long as they didn't catch her doing it. But we can't fool God. We can't worship Him on Sunday and then worship money the rest of the week. People who run their businesses on Christian principles get reputations in the community for being honest and ethical, which makes others want to do business with them. Even worldly minded people automatically expect Christians to be honest. Nothing can ruin a Christian's testimony faster than being known as a deceitful businessperson. Zaccheus, a tax collector, started out worshipping money. Then he met Jesus face-to-face and had an immediate change of character. Not only did Zaccheus stop worshipping money, but he actually gave back money that he had stolen from people. You can bet people wanted to know the Person who made such a change in Zaccheus.

We want others to see Jesus in our business practices as well as our lives.

"I'm a Train"

Don't live any longer the way this world lives. Let your way of thinking be completely changed. Then you will be able to test what God wants for you. And you will agree that what he wants is right. His plan is good and pleasing and perfect.
ROMANS 12:2 NIrV

A three-year-old boy decided he was Thomas the Tank Engine.
He would only wear blue clothes
and insisted everyone call him, "Thomas."
One day in a store, a woman said to the boy's mother,
"What a darling little boy."
Indignantly the boy said, "I'm a train!"

God gives us some fascinating challenges. One of them is determining the difference between our roles singly as well as corporately. God created each one of us not only individually but to be an individual. We each have a unique purpose to fulfill in the Kingdom of God. The apostle Paul gave a good analogy to help us understand this challenge. Each part of the body of Christ has its own job to perform to keep the whole body healthy (see 1 Corinthians 12:11-20). Understanding God's plan for our lives as individuals helps us understand our role in His overall design. How can we know God's plan for us? Romans 12:2 gives us the answer: By renewing our mind with a Christlike attitude. For when God guides our thinking, we will be conformed to His perfect plan and become the person He created us to be.

God's plan for us is perfect.

"Need a Time-Out"

*These commandments that I give you today are to be on your
hearts. Impress them on your children. Talk about them when you sit
at home and when you walk along the road,
when you lie down and when you get up.*
DEUTERONOMY 6:6–7 NIV

*A four-year-old girl watched her mother get angry
and yell at someone on the phone.
When her mother had slammed the phone down, the girl said to her,
"Mommy, you need a time-out."*

Sometimes our children can bring us up short. We might not realize how what we are doing is impressing them. Hopefully, like the child in the story, they will correct our bad and imitate our good behavior. Fortunately, God is very proactive. He knows that if we are doing what He wants and has told us to do, we won't have time to stray off the path. That is why He commanded us to impress our children with His commandments. The word *impress* means to produce a mark by applying pressure. The pressure we apply here is the constant talking about God's commandments. The mark we want to produce is an invisible but important one. We want to make an unforgettable memory in our children's minds. We want them to grow up remembering and obeying the Lord's commandments. Then they can teach them to their own children.

We impress our children every day with all we do and all we say.

"Shaving the Cat"

But he rejected the advice which the elders had given him,
and consulted the young men who had grown up with him.
1 KINGS 12:8 NKJV

A mother came into the bathroom to find her four-year-old son
squirting shaving cream onto the family cat.
"What are you doing?" the mother asked.
"I'm shaving the cat," her son replied.
"Why in the world would you want to shave the cat?"
the mother asked.
" 'Cause Billy told me to," her son replied.

Peer pressure is a strong influence in our children's lives and ours as well. We want to surround our children and ourselves with positive peers who will influence us for good and not evil. When Solomon died, his son Rehoboam became king. The people came to Rehoboam and asked him to lighten the burden of service Solomon had imposed upon them. Rehoboam told them to come back in three days, while he considered the matter. First he consulted with the elders who had advised Solomon. They told Rehoboam to lighten the people's load. But he didn't like their advice. So he consulted with his friends. They told him to assert his authority and show the people who was king. Rehoboam liked their advice. When the people came back the third day, Rehoboam told them that he was going to make their burden even heavier than Solomon had. As a result, the kingdom of Israel split with ten tribes following Jeroboam and only two tribes staying with Rehoboam. Listening to bad advice from his peers lost Rehoboam most of his kingdom.

The best advice is God's advice.

"The City of Babylon"

External religious worship [religion as it is expressed in outward acts] that is pure and unblemished in the sight of God the Father is this: to visit and help and care for the orphans and widows in their affliction and need, and to keep oneself unspotted and uncontaminated from the world.

JAMES 1:27 AMP

*A family was riding a Ferris wheel at a county fair.
When they were at the top of the ride,
their four-year-old son exclaimed,
"I can see the whole city of Babylon from here!"*

The world around us creeps in on us more than we know. It is subtle. We have to keep our guard up. "Everybody's doing it" is not a viable excuse for us or our children. If we could be above the world, looking down, we could see "the whole city of Babylon" and avoid it. But because we are eye level with that city, it sometimes doesn't look all that bad to us. One way to keep the world from creeping in on us is to keep our eyes fixed on the heavenly city—the New Jerusalem (see Revelation 21:2). When we compare the two places, we can instantly see what is wrong with the worldly Babylon. By helping those less fortunate, we will become unblemished in the sight of God our Father—unspotted and uncontaminated from this world.

**Nothing in the city of Babylon can compare to
what awaits us in the New Jerusalem.**

"We Do Not Behave Like That"

[Love] does not behave rudely,
does not seek its own, is not provoked.
1 CORINTHIANS 13:5 NKJV

While watching a cartoon character run around
knocking things over and making a mess,
a three-year-old told his nanny, "We do not behave like that."

We want our children to be well behaved. So, when they witness someone behaving badly and say things like this boy did, our hearts are overjoyed. For it is then that we realize we are having a good influence on them and are raising them correctly. But what about us? Are we showing our children exemplary behavior? Little ones are very quick to pick up on things. The do-as-I-say-and-not-as-I-do philosophy has little or no effect on our children because they watch what we do much more than they ever listen to what we say. So when they see us loving our neighbors, they'll know that they should love their neighbors. When they see us sharing the Gospel, they'll want to do the same. It is uncanny and a little scary how much our children imitate us. God put us here to be good examples, as well as good teachers and good parents, to our children. Let us be careful how we instruct these wonderful little bundles of joy that God has blessed us with.

Our children are following in our footsteps.
Let's make sure our footsteps lead them to the Lord.

"Bad Hair Day"

Consider it pure joy, my brothers and sisters,
whenever you face trials of many kinds.
JAMES 1:2 NIV

A father watched his five-year-old daughter come into the living room.
Usually a happy child, this day she was distressed.
"What's the matter, honey?" the father asked.
With a sigh, the child replied,
"Daddy, I'm having a really bad hair day."

If bad hair was all that went wrong for us on any given day, we'd probably rejoice. But we need to realize that although we may think another's troubles are minor compared to ours, our troubles may be minor compared to someone else's. It helps to consider some examples of people in the Bible, who experienced suffering. Because they refused to bow down to an idol, Shadrach, Meshach, and Abednego were thrown into a fiery furnace. The interesting thing is they didn't come out until Nebuchadnezzar commanded them to. Why? Because Jesus was in the fire with them. When we're in our troubles—be they small or large—God is in there with us. Just like He was with Moses in the wilderness, with Jonah inside the big fish, and with Peter in prison—all examples of people who suffered but counted on God to see them through. It stands to reason that we can't help others to trust God through their troubles until we've trusted Him through ours. Having a bad day? Take heart. Trust God.

Count it all joy when the Father gives you a test.
Count it all joy because He's making you His best.

Enjoying God's Creatures

You have made him to have dominion over the works of Your hands;
You have put all things under his feet, all sheep and oxen—even the
beasts of the field, the birds of the air, and the fish of the sea.
PSALM 8:6–8 NKJV

A seven-year-old girl told her friend, "You're lucky you have cats.
They keep you giggled up."

All of God's creation is here for us to take pleasure in. Some of us especially enjoy the animals we have as pets. Most pet owners have funny stories about the antics of their animals or heart-warming ones about how a dog rescued them or how a cat warned them of a fire. God gave us His creatures to take care of and when we take care of them, God blesses us. Some nursing homes have discovered the value of letting their patients have regular access to dogs and cats. Although the animals don't live in the home, they are kept in kennels nearby. On certain days, the animals are brought in so that patients can hold, pet, feed, and enjoy the comfort of loving one of God's creatures. We can also enjoy God's wild animals. Seeing squirrels play tag on a tree, a starling taking a bath, or a hawk floating effortlessly above us in the sky can remind us of all the good things God created for us to enjoy. What a wonderful world this is! Rejoice!

It's important for us to enjoy things that keep us "giggled up."
God's creatures can do just that.

"FLOAT YOUR BOAT"

"You shall rejoice in all to which you have put your hand, you and your households, in which the LORD your God has blessed you."
DEUTERONOMY 12:7 NKJV

Watching her nanny doing housework,
a seven-year-old girl asked what she could do to help.
"Honey," said the nanny, if you will just fold the washcloths
and towels, that would really float my boat."
The little girl began folding the laundry.
In a short while, she said, "I'm done.
You can come float your boat now."

Little tasks can seem so annoying and time consuming, especially if they are repetitive. But the Bible says we are to "do all to the glory of God" (1 Corinthians 10:31 NKJV). Maybe we envy those who seem to have the terrific spiritual jobs like preaching, teaching, and being missionaries. But God has always blessed the littlest task that we do for Him. And even if it's in our home where nobody sees but us, we know that God sees. What we might consider too small to notice, God notices. Every duty that we do is for Him, in His name and for His glory. And remember, it is God who gave us these small things to do in the first place. As we faithfully and joyfully do our little chores, God is preparing us for whatever He has for us yet to come. His "Well done, thou good and faithful servant" (Matthew 25:21 KJV) was said to the man with two talents as well as to the man with five.

When we are focused on giving God the glory,
even folding laundry can float our boat.

"GUESS WHAT, GOD?"

You will fill me with joy when I am with you.
You will give me endless pleasures at your right hand.
PSALM 16:11 NIrV

A four-year-old boy was saying his nightly prayers.
He started, "Now I lay me down to sleep. . .and guess what, God?
I'm getting rollerblades for Christmas!"

Enthusiasm comes from the Greek *entheos*, which means "God in us." Because we have God in us, we should be enthusiastic about all the things we receive from Him. We are usually quite willing to take our sorrows and worries to the Lord. How about sharing our excitements and joys with Him, too? Although God is lovingly concerned about our troubles, He also enthusiastically rejoices in our joys. Thankfulness and praise are the sacrifices God wants most from His people. Every day He gives us gorgeous sunrises and sunsets, as well as homes, cars, and other blessings we just take in stride. He also gives us our children to delight in. And just as we enjoy sharing in our children's happiness, God enjoys sharing in ours, especially since it all comes from Him. When our children say, "Guess what?" we say, "What?" When we say, "Guess what, God?" He says, "What?" And then listens happily to our answer. Like this little boy, we need to enthusiastically share with God what is important to us. After all, God enthusiastically shared with us what was most important to Him—His only begotten Son.

God is waiting to rejoice with us—today and every day!

JESUS DOWN THE CHIMNEY

*Blessed be the Lord, who daily bears our burden,
the God who is our salvation.*
PSALM 68:19 NASB

*When asked if he knew what Christmas was all about,
a three-year-old boy said, "That's when Jesus comes down the chimney."*

Thank God we're not confused about the message of Christmas. Joy does not depend on the world and how it sees or celebrates Christmas. We know its true meaning. God gave us good tidings of great joy—wondrous joy—awesome joy. Jesus didn't come down a chimney; He left His glory above and came down to bring us what we so desperately needed—salvation from our sins. We cannot even begin to imagine what Jesus left behind when He came down to earth to be born as a poor, defenseless Babe. The Bible says that He was born to die that we might live (see Hebrews 2:17). Years ago a man died while saving the life of a woman. The woman was so grateful that every year on the anniversary of the man's death, she would visit his family members and thank them again for his sacrifice. Never once did she ask them for anything else. They would have thought her most ungrateful if she had. Now look at what Psalm 68:19 says: As if salvation weren't enough all by itself, Jesus also daily bears our burdens. He not only died for us, He lives for us. The love of Jesus is indescribable. All we can do is thank Him and praise Him for it.

Joy to the world indeed!

Joyful Noise

Make a joyful noise unto the LORD, all ye lands.
PSALM 100:1 KJV

A four-year-old girl was in the church nursery where
there was a speaker so that the attendants
could hear the worship service.
When the congregation began to sing the first hymn,
the girl said in amazement, "That almost sounds like music!"

Some people have beautiful singing voices. When we listen to them, we can almost imagine what the heavenly choir is going to sound like. Some of us—whether or not in tune—just love to belt out a song. God loves music, especially that which is sung or played in praise of Him. After Solomon built the temple, singers sang at the Lord's house all day and all night (see 1 Chronicles 25; 2 Chronicles 5). The members of the group rotated shifts, but the music was constant, praising God every minute of every day. Many of the psalms are songs that were sung on various occasions, such as Passover. When Jesus and His disciples were finished with their Passover meal, they sang a song, most likely a psalm, and departed. God also appreciates music made by various instruments. David played a harp. Miriam danced with a timbrel when she sang of Israel's deliverance from Egypt. Psalm 150 has a list of instruments that God enjoys hearing. Nothing pleases Him more than singing and playing your praise to Him!

How wonderful to know that all our efforts
to please God are accepted by Him
100 percent. No "almost" about it.

"Jumpoline"

*"As soon as the sound of your greeting reached my ears,
the baby in my womb leaped for joy."*
LUKE 1:44 NIV

*A five-year-old girl came home from her friend's house
all excited about the fun they had.
"We got to jump on her Jumpoline!" she told her mother.*

Trampolines can be lots of fun. There is joy in bouncing up and down with childlike abandon. Luke 1:44 is a quote from Elizabeth when Mary came to visit her. The child in Elizabeth's womb would later be known as John the Baptist. When Elizabeth heard Mary's greeting, the baby inside her leaped with joy. Why? Because Mary was already pregnant with Baby Jesus. Even before he was born, John the Baptist knew his Messiah had come. We don't need a trampoline for our souls to leap with joy at the wonderful fact that our Messiah has arrived! Our souls can keep leaping and bounding with the joy of knowing that we have a personal relationship with Jesus Christ, our Savior. That joy in Jesus helps us to see beyond the difficulties of today to the possibilities of tomorrow. Hebrews 12:2 says that Jesus endured the cross because of the joy that was set before Him—the joy in knowing that He has conquered sin and death and created a way for us to live with Him forever. Hosanna! "Blessed is He who comes in the name of the LORD!" (Matthew 21:9 NKJV).

The joy of Jesus keeps our hearts leaping high with happiness.

Peewee Soccer

A mother was watching her five-year-old son play peewee soccer.
When it was his turn to be goalie, the boy ran out into the field and
snatched up the soccer ball. Running toward his mother, he held the
ball out to her yelling, "I got the ball! I got the ball!"
When the next child took his turn to be goalie, he also grabbed the ball
and took it to his mother crying, "I got the ball!"
Every child after that did the same thing when he or she was goalie.
At the end of the game, the first little boy said to another child
on his team, "I got the ball."
"So did I," replied the second child. And they high-fived.

When God tosses the ball of life to us, we need to grab it and take it right back to Him. He is on the sidelines and on the field, ready and waiting to hear from us. Just as we enjoy sharing our children's successes, Father God enjoys sharing ours. When others see our excitement in taking our triumphs to God, they will be encouraged to do the same. The joy in the Lord is contagious! Spread it around today!

By sharing our triumphs with God and each other,
we experience heavenly and earthly joy.

"Rain Barrel"

And whatever you do [no matter what it is] in word or deed, do everything in the name of the Lord Jesus and in [dependence upon] His Person, giving praise to God the Father through Him.
Colossians 3:17 AMP

A three-year-old boy proudly told everyone that he was going to be the rain barrel [ring bearer] at his cousin's wedding.

What we may consider insignificant, someone else might see as a great blessing. This child wasn't the star of the wedding. He wasn't the bride or groom. All that mattered to him was playing a part in the wedding—be it ever so humble. If we could see our activities through God's eyes, we would perceive that everything we do is important, not only to God but also to His plan for us and His kingdom. Nothing we do is too small for God to use for His glory. The pearl of great price began as a grain of sand that irritated an oyster. Although what we are doing may seem like just a speck to us, God can see the priceless gem it will become. Therefore, we can joyfully fulfill whatever task God asks us to do, knowing that it's important to God; He wouldn't have asked us to do it otherwise.

**If God wants us to be a "rain barrel,"
we should be the best rain barrel that we can be.**

"ROLLING ON THE FLOOR"

"The Lord your God is with you.
He is mighty enough to save you.
He will take great delight in you.
The quietness of his love will calm you down.
He will sing with joy because of you."
ZEPHANIAH 3:17 NIrV

Laughing at something her aunt had said, a six-year-old girl told her,
"That was so funny. I'm rolling on the floor here."
She then proceeded to roll on the floor.

Happiness is contagious. When someone laughs, we have a tendency to laugh with him or her. We celebrate happiness with a bride and groom on their wedding day. We rejoice with new parents over the birth of their child. But happiness is temporary, whereas joy is permanent. Joy is the fruit of the Spirit that comes because God loves us and delights in us. It is not our joy in the Lord but His joy in us that gives us the strength to carry on through good times and bad. God created us for one reason—to bring Him pleasure. So if we have pleased God this week, we have fulfilled our reason for existing. Luke 15:10 says that the angels rejoice when someone accepts Jesus. How wonderful to know that we can bring joy to God and His angels—in the blessings He gives us and simply by accepting His most wonderful gift: Jesus.

We are the delight of God.

Who Liked Your Dress?

Keep your lives free from the love of money and be content
with what you have, because God has said,
"Never will I leave you; never will
I forsake you." So we say with confidence, "The Lord is my helper;
I will not be afraid. What can mere mortals do to me?"
HEBREWS 13:5–6 NIV

Very proud of her new dress, a ten-year-old girl couldn't wait to
wear it to church. After services, her grandmother said,
"Well, did anyone like your new dress?"
"Yes," the girl replied.
"Who?" asked her grandmother.
"Me," said the girl.

The Hebrews writer gives us the secret to joy—knowing the
Lord is our helper and will always be by our side—no matter
what! All else pales in comparison. This leads us to joyfilled contentment with what we have because we know that
material things are only temporary and that our loving God
gives us only what we need. In return, God wants us to have
an attitude of gratitude for all His wondrous blessings. When
truly grateful, we won't care about other people's opinions. Nor
will we be discontent. When we give our children something,
we want them to be thankful and joyful. God knows that and
He wants us to teach that to our children. The opposite of joy
is discontent. Instead of whining about things we don't have, we
need to take joy in the things we do have.

Joy comes from being content with all the things God has given us.

"Cart Weasels"

*All scripture is given by inspiration of God, and is profitable for
doctrine, for reproof, for correction, for instruction in righteousness:
that the man of God may be perfect,
thoroughly furnished unto all good works.*
2 TIMOTHY 3:16–17 KJV

*An eight-year-old girl said to her mother, "Come watch me.
I'm going to do cart weasels [cartwheels] on the lawn."*

Reading about the people in the Bible shows us the way God worked with our forefathers, how He treated them and delivered them from all their troubles. Their stories reveal that God, who sees the big picture, knows what's best. This knowledge allows us to do joyfilled spiritual "cart weasels" when we are in dire straits of our own. Consider Job who, in one fell swoop, lost his property and children, and later, his health. Although Job had no idea why he had so many troubles all at once, by reading his story, we can see that God was showing him off, using him to silence Satan. And in the end, God "blessed the latter days of Job more than his beginning" (Job 42:12 NKJV), providing him with more property and children. We may have no idea why we have trials and difficulties, but we do know God is using us to work His awesome plan. That fact gives us joy and that joy gives us the strength to endure as God works His will through us.

**When we truly believe that God knows what's best,
then we know whatever comes our way
is an occasion for us to rejoice.**

LEARNING

Knowing More Than Anyone Else

Don't think of yourself more highly than you should.

After his first day at kindergarten,
a five-year-old boy expressed to his mother his disgust with his teacher.
"Do you know that you can't just talk to that woman?
You have to raise your hand.
And she didn't even know what an apple was. I had to tell her."

In the verse above, Paul was telling Christians that we are to not to live the way the world lives. Instead, we are to live in the good, acceptable, and perfect will of God and not become all puffed up with our spirituality. To do that, our focus cannot be on us, but on our Lord. A man who had survived a horrible flood spent the rest of his life telling his story to anyone who came within earshot. When he finally died and went to heaven, he asked God if he could find an audience so he could tell his flood story again. God let him do just that. When the crowd was assembled, God said to the man, "I just want you to know—Noah is in the audience." No matter what we think we know, someone else knows more. The more spiritually mature we are, the more humble we become as we realize just how much we still have to learn.

It is impossible stand pridefully before the throne of God.

Leaning on Our Own Understanding

Trust in the LORD with all your heart,
and lean not on your own understanding.
PROVERBS 3:5 NKJV

A four-year-old boy asked his mother, "Why can't chickens fly?"
"Because that's the way God made them," his mother replied.
"No," he said, "it's because their wings are too small."

The trouble with leaning on our own understanding is that most of the time we don't really recognize what the problem really is. And while we are trying to figure it out by ourselves, we aren't trusting God to solve the problem for us. Even if what God prompts us to do doesn't make sense to us, we should follow the Lord's leading. It's tempting to think that we can come up with our own solutions, but that inevitably leads to more trouble. God promised Abraham and Sarah a son but Sarah got tired of waiting, so she gave Abraham her maidservant Hagar. According to the custom of that day, a barren wife could give her maidservant to her husband and any child that resulted would be considered the wife's. But when Hagar was expecting, she became arrogant toward Sarah, making the latter even more aware of her barrenness. In a fit of jealousy, Sarah made Abraham send Hagar away. We all know who Hagar's descendants are— the Arabs. Having leaned on her own understanding, Sarah started a war that lasts to this very day. Let's not follow in her footsteps. Need a solution to a problem? Patiently await God's answer.

God is the one who truly knows all.
Lean on His understanding.

LEARNING BY REPETITION

"This Book of the Law shall not depart from your mouth, but you shall meditate in it day and night, that you may observe to do according to all that is written in it. For then you will make your way prosperous, and then will you have good success."
JOSHUA 1:8 NKJV

A three-year-old boy was learning words the way most three-year-olds do—by repeating the same word over and over again.
One day when he had said the same word too many times,
his nanny said, "Okay. That's enough."
"That's enough?" the boy said.
"Enough? Is that enough? That's enough."
He kept repeating the word enough until his nanny finally said,
"Okay. That's enough of enough."

In Joshua 1:8, the word *meditate* means to mutter out loud over and over. Think of all the songs we know by heart because we have sung them over and over again. We learn by repeating things, by rereading them until their meaning is clear to us, providing us with greater insight about God and ourselves. Speaking Bible verses out loud not only helps us to concentrate on what we are learning but allows the verses to take root within and without, for God says, "My word…shall not return to Me void" (Isaiah 55:11 NKJV). And be sure to pay attention when the Bible repeats things. Chances are that if God says something more than once, it's important.

Every time we read the Bible, we gain new insights into who God is and how He wants us to live.

LEARNING FROM EXPERIENCE

My heart had great experience of wisdom and knowledge.
ECCLESIASTES 1:16 KJV

A two-year-old boy walked into the kitchen and said to his mother,
"Christmas trees taste yucky."

We would like our children to learn from our experiences, thus saving them the trouble of learning things the hard way. Although King Solomon was and still is considered to be one of the wisest men who ever lived, he himself learned things the hard way. The book of Ecclesiastes is his journey through life as Solomon, experiencing all the pleasures the world has to offer, discovers they are empty and vain. Unfortunately, he didn't learn from the experiences of his father, David, nor from those of Israel as a nation. But he did finally come to the right conclusion. Solomon sums up all the lessons he learned in the next to last verse of Ecclesiastes: "Let us hear the conclusion of the whole matter: Fear God, and keep his commandments: for this is the whole duty of man" (12:13 KJV). We don't have to be foolish but can learn from Solomon's experiences. The world hasn't changed. As Solomon so aptly put it, "There is nothing new under the sun" (Ecclesiastes 1:9 NIV). All the fleshly, material experiences he had didn't gratify him one bit. They won't gratify us either. The only satisfaction we have in this life comes from fearing God and keeping His commandments.

We can learn from Solomon's experiences.

LEARNING THE RIGHT THING

Study to shew thyself approved unto God, a workman that needeth
not to be ashamed, rightly dividing the word of truth.
2 TIMOTHY 2:15 KJV

When asked what he was learning in Sunday school,
a two-year-old boy replied, "Be quiet."

Because we want our children to get a good education, we're concerned about what they learn in grade school. But how concerned are we about what they are learning in Sunday school? Are they getting a good biblical education? The verse above says we are to study so that we can rightly divide the Word of God. That means that we are to examine God's Word so that we can understand what He is trying to tell us and also so that we can expose false teachers. False teachers are those who try to use God's word to support their own erroneous beliefs. The Bible tells us the way to identity false teachers is by seeing if their words are true. If they aren't, they are not speaking God's truth. As we rightly divide God's word, it will in turn divide us. Hebrews 4:12 says that God's Word is sharper than a two-edged sword, dividing soul and spirit. Why would God's word deem to separate our inner workings? Because our soul is where our emotions are and our spirit is where God's truth resides. Our emotions (feelings) are not to color our interpretation of God's Word. Instead, we must allow God's Spirit to teach our spirits His truth.

The more we study God's word, the more God gives us to study.

Learning to Listen

And behold, the LORD passed by, and a great and strong wind tore into the mountains. . .but the LORD was not in the wind; and after the wind an earthquake, but the LORD was not in the earthquake; and after the earthquake a fire, but the LORD was not in the fire; and after the fire a still small voice.

1 KINGS 19:11–12 NKJV

A four-year-old girl delighted in telling lengthy prince and princess stories.
Her family had taken to listening to her with half an ear.
One day when she was telling a story to her grandmother, the girl suddenly stopped. Thinking that the story was done, the grandmother said, "That was a good story."
"I wasn't done," the four-year-old said indignantly.
"Oh, I'm sorry," her grandmother apologized. "Please tell me the rest."
The little girl thought for a moment and then said, "The end."

Sometimes when we're busy or involved in something, we may listen to our children with half an ear. But in doing so, we might miss something they say that's really important. The same is true of our communication with God. When we get too busy, not taking time to stop and really listen to what God wants to tell us, we may miss out on something important. God wants you to talk and then listen to Him, just as He listens, then talks to us. So we must tune out life's great winds, earthquakes, and fires, and open both ears to God. What He whispers will change our lives.

Don't get distracted by all the noise;
listen, instead, for the still, small voice.

Ancient Wisdom

With the ancient is wisdom; and in length of days understanding.
JOB 12:12 KJV

A woman took her grandchildren to
the museum at Fort Benning, Georgia.
"This building used to be the hospital," she told them,
"and I was born in that hospital."
Her six-year-old grandson looked at her and said,
"Granny, I knew you were old but I didn't know
your were a museum piece!"

Matthew 10:16 says we are to be as wise as serpents and as harmless as doves. But we are not to be wise in our own eyes (see Proverbs 3:7). The Bible warns us time and again about not getting ourselves "puffed up" (1 Corinthians 13:4 KJV) about what we know (see Romans 12:16). We can't let our minds go to our heads. Yet we are to obtain and maintain a heart of wisdom (see Psalm 90:12). The book of Proverbs is full of good advice on how to do this. Basically it says that we must seek after wisdom (see Proverbs 2:4). Wisdom isn't just learning and knowledge. It doesn't automatically come with age. But as we get older we should get wiser. So, as we grow in experience year after year, we should be able to make practical applications of the learning and knowledge we have acquired. James 1:5 gives us a wonderful suggestion—if we lack wisdom, all we have to do is ask God to give it to us, and He will.

The Ancient of Days has all the wisdom we will ever need,
and He's very willing to share it with us.

Sweating Eyes

Jesus saw the crowds. So he went up on a mountainside
and sat down. His disciples came to him.
Then he began to teach them.
MATTHEW 5:1–2 NIrV

A five-year-old girl saw a lady who was crying.
"Look, Mama," she said, "that lady's eyes are sweating."

When trying to describe something to someone, we try to put things in terms we can understand. When Jesus taught people, He used illustrations of everyday things that were familiar to them—a farmer sowing seed, lost sheep, vineyards, and others. The people who heard His teachings were amazed at how well they could understand Him. They came from miles around to follow Jesus and listen to what He said. When Jesus began to teach them, He sat down on a mountainside. In the culture of that day, if a rabbi was going to preach, he stood; but if he was going to teach or to explain something, he sat down. The Bible says that the crowds were astonished at His teachings (see Matthew 7:28) because He didn't teach like the scribes or Pharisees who were fond of arguing over minute points in the Torah. Jesus simply explained God's great kingdom was at hand and then described that kingdom in terms the people could understand. Instead of trying to impress someone with His rhetoric, Jesus impressed upon them the love of God.

Like Jesus, we are to spread the Good News in such a
way that people can understand its message.

"The *E* Word"

*Let no foul or polluting language, nor evil word nor unwholesome or
worthless talk [ever] come out of your mouth, but only such [speech]
as is good and beneficial to the spiritual progress of others, as is
fitting to the need and the occasion, that it may be a blessing and
give grace (God's favor) to those who hear it.*
EPHESIANS 4:29 AMP

*A six-year-old girl told her mother, "Shannon said the E word."
Her mother racked her brain but couldn't think of any naughty word
that started with E. Finally she said to her daughter,
"Just this once, tell me what the E word is."
"Idiot," the little girl replied.*

Idiot is not a very nice word, but we don't usually think of it as
a swear word. Yet God says any word that is not uplifting and
beneficial is one that doesn't need to be spoken. We are here
to encourage and help others—no matter what we think about
them or their behavior. Yet our attitude about them can affect
our speech and actions. If we think someone is an idiot, we're
not going to be too concerned about uplifting or encouraging
that person. But we must recognize that words are powerful,
especially those spoken, so our speech should be loving and
compassionate. When talking to someone, let's consider what
Jesus would say. Maybe if we can look beyond our perception of
someone as an idiot, we will see the person as God does.

Our words must reflect the heart and mind of Jesus.

Finished?

Whatever your hand finds to do, do it with all your might.
ECCLESIASTES 9:10 NIV

A five-year-old boy came home from kindergarten
and told his mother that he didn't have to go to school anymore.
Surprised, she asked him why not.
"We learned Z today," he said.

God created each one of us to do a specific task to further His plan and His kingdom. And He equipped us with the necessary talents and gifts to accomplish that task. Only Esther could save her people from complete annihilation. Only Paul could open the door of salvation to the Gentiles. Only Solomon could build the temple. Only Elijah could rout the prophets of Baal. Only Abraham and Sarah could have the child of promise, Isaac. Only Bezalel could build and furnish the Tabernacle in the wilderness. A divine plan of life is continuously unfolding for each of us. Great peace of mind comes in knowing that we are using our God-given talents for the purpose God intended. Our lives are about being who God created us to be. He delights in what we are doing for Him—from *A* to *Z*. So we mustn't let other people distract us from our purpose or talk us into thinking our task is completed. We're not finished until God says we are.

If we're still on this earth,
we haven't finished what God put us here to do.

NAMES ARE IMPORTANT

*So God lifted him up to the highest place. He gave him the name
that is above every name. When the name of Jesus is spoken,
everyone's knee will bow to worship him. . . .
Everyone's mouth will say that Jesus Christ is Lord.
And God the Father will receive the glory.*
PHILIPPIANS 2:9–11 NIrV

*A seven-year-old girl was telling her Sunday school class
the story of the Jesus' trial. She said, "And then Jesus had to go
before that man, what was his name? Oh, yeah, Punch Pilate."*

Philippians 2:10 says that when the name *Jesus* is spoken, every
knee will bow. Jesus won't even have to be there in person. Just
the mention of His name will bring everyone to their knees.
Jesus is the most powerful name that ever was, is, or will be.
Romans 10:13 says whoever "calls on the name of the Lord will
be saved" (NIrV). Now *that's* power. None of our names has that
kind of authority. A man went into a bank to cash a check.
"Do you have an account here?" the teller asked. "No," said
the man, "but my name is the same as the owner of this bank.
He's my father." Our names identify the families we belong to.
Many people trace their family lineage, hoping to find a famous
ancestor. But we believers don't need to research our genealogies
to seek a forebear of renown, because we belong to the family
of the person with the most famous and powerful name there
is—Jesus!

There is no better name than Jesus.

"A Beautiful Child"

Dear friends, now we are children of God.
1 JOHN 3:2 NIV

A three-year-old boy got used to people commenting on his looks.
One day when his mother was at the store,
the boy said to the checkout clerk,
"My name is Edward, and I'm a beautiful child."

Oh, if we could only see ourselves as God sees us. Imagine what He considered when He first dreamed us up. Imagine what He created our lives to be. God sees each one of us as His beautiful child. And He gives us the right to boldly come into His presence with our praises and petitions. He graciously listens to us, just like we listen to our children. The Bible says that we look on people's outward appearance but God looks at everyone's heart (see 1 Samuel 16:7). We tell ourselves and our children that inner beauty is more important than outward beauty, and that's true. But consider this: God created everyone, their physical being as well as their spiritual being. What we think of as ugly, God thinks of as beautiful. Nothing is unsightly to Him, except sin. So no matter what our appearance, if we let the beauty of Jesus be seen in us, the world won't see anything else.

We are all God's beautiful children.

"A Moment of Silent Affection"

For with the heart one believes unto righteousness,
and with the mouth confession is made unto salvation.
ROMANS 10:10 NKJV

A six-year-old girl proudly led her first grade class
in the Pledge of Allegiance.
When they finished, she said,
"Please pause for a moment of silent affection."

There is no way to measure how much God loves us. But think about this:

The greatest heart in the universe was broken over me—
The Father sent His only Son to die upon the tree.
He saved my soul from sin's dark night and set my spirit free.
The greatest heart in the universe was broken over me.

God was heartbroken over our sin and disobedience. He wanted and needed a way to be able to forgive us and bring us back to Him. So He did the only thing He could—He provided us with the sinless, spotless Savior we needed. How do we repay this great love? How do we show God the love He shows us? How do we appreciate Jesus' overwhelming sacrifice? By literally singing His praises all day long. God calls that the sacrifice of praise and it pleases Him. We could never even begin to comprehend the magnitude of God's love for us. But we can certainly show Him our appreciation.

Upon reflection, perhaps our affection shouldn't be silent.

Finding True Love

For God so loved the world that He gave His only begotten Son,
that whoever believes in Him should not perish
but have everlasting life.
JOHN 3:16 NKJV

A four-year-old boy got a piece of peppermint candy and said,
"I like spicy candy—it makes me fall in love!"

We will never know a truer love than that of God for us. John 3:16 is perhaps the most quoted verse in the Bible. But we don't want to let our familiarity of this verse make us complacent about its tremendous message. One way to make the message of this verse more vital is to make it personal. So read it again and put yourself into it: For God so loved YOU that He gave His only begotten Son for YOU so that if YOU believe in Him YOU will not perish but YOU will have everlasting life. Is this not amazing? God loves us. We need to repeat this to ourselves throughout the day. It will change our lives, our thinking, and our behavior. God loves us so we can love others. God loves us so we can love ourselves. God loves us so we can love Him right back and show that love in our respectful obedience to His will. God loves us like no one else ever could. God loves us more than anything. Say to yourself, "God loves me." Now believe it and live it.

No one ever loved and cared for us like Jesus.

"Good Tidings"

*Then the angel said to them, "Do not be afraid, for behold,
I bring you good tidings of great joy which will be to all people."*
LUKE 2:10 NKJV

*A four-year-old boy was performing his own version of
"We Wish You a Merry Christmas."
He sang, "Good tidings we bring to you and your kids."*

Sometimes our children's interpretations are better than the original. We want to bring God's good tidings to everyone—and their kin, including kids. The love of God is evident in that He is good to all—Jew or Gentile, slave or free, male or female (see Galatians 3:28). The angel said the good tidings of Jesus' birth, of our Messiah's arrival, would bring great joy to all people, not just God's chosen people, the Israelites. God had wanted the people of Israel to be His shining light to everyone around them. Instead they drew themselves together and despised the people they referred to as "Gentile dogs." God wants us to spread His love to one and all. He doesn't want us to keep it to ourselves. Judging others is easy—having compassion for them is not. This is why we should pray for our friends *and* foes. If we are busy retaliating, we are missing the point of what God is trying to do in our lives. God has given us faith, hope, and love to share. But only love will last forever—because God is love.

God loves all people through us.

He Knows Our Names

*"I will give him a white stone with a new name engraved
on the stone, which no one knows or understands
except he who receives it."*
REVELATION 2:17 AMP

*After a visit to Santa Claus, a five-year-old boy asked his mother,
"Why did Santa ask me my name?
Shouldn't he already know who I am?"*

We don't have to introduce ourselves to God. He already knows very well who we are—right down to the number of hairs on our heads (see Matthew 10:30). Our names are not just written in His Book of Life (see Luke 10:20) but are written in His Book of Love. How wonderful for us. He not only created us, He knows us inside out, and He is interested in everything we say or do. Malachi 3:16 says, "Then those who feared the LORD talked with each other, and the LORD listened and heard. A scroll of remembrance was written in his presence concerning those who feared the LORD and honored his name" (NIV). God listens to us as we talk with each other about His awesome works. He has a Book of Remembrance where He records what we say to each other about Him. God is vitally interested in us. We are His children and He loves us unconditionally. And He already has our new names all picked out!

God loves each one of us as if we were His only child.

"I Love Jesus"

We love him because He first loved us.
1 JOHN 4:19 NKJV

*As a mother was trying to correct her four-year-old son,
he looked up at her and said,
"I love Jesus. Do you love Jesus?"*

When we go before God after we've made a mistake, we can say, "I know I did wrong, but I do love Jesus," and God immediately forgives our misdeed. Our love for Jesus and His love for us covers a multitude of sins. That's because we are covered by Jesus' righteousness. When God looks at us, He sees the finished work of His beloved Son and He remembers our sins no more (see Hebrews 8:12). God not only loves us completely, He loves us first—before we even know who He is. He loves us whether we love Him or not. We humans are not capable of this kind of love. All we can do is love Jesus just as much as we can, in every way we can. When God sees that, He loves us even more. His love for us and our love for Him make us want to do everything we can to please Him. "Give thanks to the greatest God of all. His faithful love continues forever" (Psalm 136:2 NIrv).

**No mistake we've ever made is bigger than God's love
and His power to fix it for us.**

"Just Take One"

"I have come that they may have life,
and that they may have it more abundantly."
JOHN 10:10 NKJV

A grandmother brought out her cookie jar
and asked her four-year-old grandson if he wanted a cookie.
"What do you say?" his mother prompted.
"Just take one," he replied.

God never tells us, "Just take one." In reality we don't deserve anything. But God loves us so much that He wants us to have abundantly joyful lives. Jesus, as our Good Shepherd, leads us to places of nourishment and refreshment. He doesn't give them to us begrudgingly. He doesn't tell us we can only have one or the other, but blesses us with abundance. Sometimes we might not see the good in what God sends our way, but we can trust in His love for us and know that if He sent it, it is good for us. Sometimes we might feel that we should limit ourselves to just one good thing, that maybe that's more than we should even have. But God doesn't see it that way. Just like we want our children to have all the good things they need and even want, God desires us to have what we need and sometimes what we want. It's all good and in limitless supply! So ask in love—and you will receive all God has for you!

There are no limits to the love and goodness of God.

LOVING YOURSELF

*"'You shall love the LORD your God with all your heart,
with all your soul, and with all your mind.' This is the first
and great commandment. And the second is like it:
'You shall love your neighbor as yourself.'"*
MATTHEW 22:37–40 NKJV

*While driving down the highway, a mother heard her
five-year-old daughter singing softly to herself in the backseat.
The little girl was singing a song she had made up:
"I love Mommy. I love Daddy. I love Grandma. I love Papa.
And I love myself. Yes, I love myself."*

The verse above says we are to love our neighbors *as* ourselves—
not instead of ourselves, not above ourselves, but as much as we
love ourselves. This love isn't the conceited self-love of the world
but the agape kind of love with which God loves us. Because
we know God showers us with that patient, kind, trusting,
truthful, enduring, unselfish, and hopeful kind of love, we can
love ourselves just as we are—and others, just as they are. We are
directed to love God first, our neighbors second, and ourselves
last but not least. How do we love ourselves? By patiently
allowing ourselves time to find out who we are and why God
created us and by not allowing others to put us down because
God didn't create us to live dejected lives. When we let the love
and joy of God flow through us as we love ourselves and others,
we can then teach our children how to love themselves as God
loves them.

Jesus, Others, and You—what a wonderful way to spell JOY.

"Not Her Type"

Who are you to judge someone else's servant?
To their own master, servants stand or fall.
And they will stand, for the Lord is able to make them stand.
ROMANS 14:4 NIV

An eight-year-old girl told her grandmother,
"Miss Judy's new boyfriend is not her type."
"Not her type?" her grandmother said. "What do you mean?"
"He has red hair," the girl replied.

At first, Romans 14:4 may seem negative. But when we read the entire verse we see the positive. Not only are we not to judge others, but we don't have to worry about them judging us, because God is our master and He will stand up for us. Love precludes judging. When we love others as God loves us, we want to see all their good sides. We defend them if others are judging them. Although we may not see what someone sees in someone else, we can't deny his or her right to see it. There is a part of God inside every person He created. If we can find that part, then we can love that person. So it is up to us to look as hard as we can to see God in others. After all, we are all God's servants. So who are we to judge? That's God's job.

We're all God's type.

SHOWING GOD WE LOVE HIM

*And what does the LORD require of you but to do justly,
to love mercy, and to walk humbly with your God?*
MICAH 6:8 NKJV

*A five–year-old girl was eating a pickle.
After every bite, she would lay the pickle down
and wipe her hands on her jeans.
"Use your napkin," her mother admonished her.
"It's only pickle juice," the girl replied.*

What "It's only. . ." do we use to avoid doing God's will God's way? We have our own ideas about how things should be done. Sometimes, perhaps instead of following God's clear instructions, we might look for a loophole so we can do something our way. God has already shown us how much He loves us. He asks us to show our love for Him by doing things His way. He wants us to live by faith, not by sight. He wants us to show mercy to others as He showed mercy to us. He wants us to walk humbly with Him—not running ahead to where we want to go. And why does God want all that? Because in His infinite love for us, He knows that this is how we will truly have the lives He created us to have. All we have to do is follow His perfect plan.

We show God our love through obedience.

"TOTALLY INAPPROPRIATE"

*Beloved, let us love one another, for love is of God;
and everyone who loves is born of God and knows God.*
1 JOHN 4:7 NKJV

*An eight-year-old boy overheard his grandmother singing
"I Saw Mommy Kissing Santa Claus."
Shocked, the boy said, "Granny, that is totally inappropriate.
You know Mommy can't kiss Santa Claus
because she is married to Daddy!"*

Our children have their own moral codes. They learn them from us. And whereas children are usually more rigid in their adherence to these codes, adults might have a tendency to bend the rules a little. But God's rules weren't made to be bent. The Bible condemns adultery (see Hebrews 13:4). Even children know it is wrong. God condemns it because He knows what havoc it wreaks on people. He doesn't want us to have to go through all that pain and suffering. God wants us to share His pure love with the spouse He specifically created for us to have. God intends marriage to be a model to the world of how Jesus loves the church. The unsaved world won't think much of the Bride of Christ if it sees Christians being untrue to their wedding vows. There are so many ways we witness to the world, but the one that seems to make the biggest impression is how we behave ourselves.

To show God's pure love, we must love purely.

USING LOVE

"Do not despise the chastening of the LORD,
nor be discouraged when you are rebuked by Him;
for whom the LORD loves He chastens."
HEBREWS 12:5–6 NKJV

A mother was correcting her four-year-old son
when he looked at her and said, "I love you, Mommy."
"I love you, too," she replied. "That's why I won't allow you
to behave like that."

Our children will often use whatever means available to try to distract us when we are disciplining them. We may tend to do the same thing with God. Perhaps we feel that the situation we are in is a form of punishment. Then we might try to bargain our way out of it, even if we feel we deserve a chastising from God. Consider this: As harsh as it seemed to the Israelites whenever God chastened them, it was nothing compared to what He did to their enemies. Most of the nations we read about in the Old Testament no longer exist. God wiped them out completely. So the next time we feel we are perhaps being chastened by the Lord a little too severely, we need to remember two things: (1) He loves us, so He will never hurt us; and (2) if we think we have it bad, we need to look at the demise of God's enemies. Then, instead of bargaining with God, we can be grateful that we are His children and He loves us enough to keep us on His path.

God is love, and He uses His love to correct our misdeeds.

"Where Are You?"

Then the LORD God called to Adam and said to him,
"Where are you?"
GENESIS 3:9 NKJV

A mother was frantically searching for her three-year-old son.
She called and called him but he wouldn't answer.
Finally she went to the back door and called,
"Jack, are you in the woods?"
"Yes," came the answer.
"You know you aren't allowed in the woods," the mother called.
"You get back here right now." "No," said the little voice,
"because you will spank me."

Fear of the Lord doesn't mean being afraid of Him or being afraid that He will punish us. Fear of the Lord means being afraid to do anything that would hurt or grieve Him. But if we have done something wrong, we don't have to try to hide from God like Adam did. We can go boldly to Him and confess our wrongdoing, knowing that He will not only forgive us but forget our sin. God created us in His image and likeness. He has placed within us His Spirit. Even if we try to hide, we are never alone because God will never leave us. We don't have to be afraid of what He will do to us. Instead, we can take comfort in the fact that no matter what we do, God loves us unconditionally and He always will.

Love never fails because God is love,
and He never fails in His love toward us.

PEACE

Busy, Busy, Busy

Fear ye not, stand still, and see the salvation of the LORD,
which he will shew to you to day.
EXODUS 14:13 KJV

A four-year-old girl watched her mother rushing around
getting ready to go to work.
"Mommy," said the girl, "you need to take a relax."

If all we show our children is hurriedness and stress, then that's what they are going to think is normal. Moses spoke the words in the verse above to the Israelites as they stood between the Egyptians and the Red Sea. Surely most of the Israelites thought they should be doing something, anything. But God said, "Stand still and see My salvation." Is God telling us to stand still? If so, are we listening to Him? Being still allows us to be centered in the presence of God. We can't watch God work if we are too busy rushing around trying to fix all our situations by ourselves. Consider Jesus. He was serene and joyful. When He was weary, He went apart and rested. He spent every morning with His Father, getting instructions for the day. Like Jesus, we can give God our to-do list and He will swap it for His list for us. God is working all things for our good and will complete the work He has begun in us. All we have to do is be still and let Him.

If our eyes are upon the Lord, He will see us through.

"God Resting"

*There remains therefore a rest for the people of God.
For he who has entered His rest has himself
also ceased from his works as God did from His.*
HEBREWS 4:9–10 NKJV

*A Sunday school class was making a timeline of the days of creation.
One seven-year-old boy handed his teacher a picture of a bunch of
clouds with a person lying on them. "What is this?" the teacher asked.
"It's God resting up in heaven," the boy replied.*

The last thing God fashioned during the seven days of creation
was rest—not because He needed it but because He knew we
did. These verses in Hebrews have a now-and-then application.
Now God gives us the rest that comes with the knowledge that
our salvation is not through any works we have done or are
doing but depends completely on Jesus and His work on our
behalf. We can rest from trying to earn salvation or blessings
or righteousness, knowing that all these things are ours through
Christ. Once we realize that Jesus did it all and still does it
all, we can rest in the knowledge that our salvation is already
complete. We do have things to do here for God's Kingdom,
but in reality, Jesus actually does them through us. So we are
still resting in Him. *Then*, after our work is finished, God will
welcome us into His rest that He has created for us to enjoy
with Him eternally.

Our hearts are restless until they rest in God.

Good Will Come

A two-year-old boy came into the house crying
and told his mother that he was hurt.
"Where did you hurt yourself?" his mother asked,
looking him over to see where the injury was.
The two-year-old pointed to the yard and said, "Over there."

No matter how we get hurt or where we get hurt, God knows what is going to happen and is already working it out for our good. If we focus on the trials of life, they can have a fearful aspect. But if we look up to the One who controls all of life's circumstances, then we have His peace. We experience the peace of God by worrying about nothing, praying about everything, and being thankful for anything that comes our way (see Philippians 4:6–7). That is God's foolproof formula for having His peace that passes all understanding. God planned a future for each one of us. He is tirelessly and lovingly looking out for our best interests. How can we be stressed when we know that God is on our side? Not only does He give us peace, but He *is* our peace.

We don't look forward in fear, but in the peaceful knowledge that God will deliver us from all our troubles.

Making Peace

Blessed are the peacemakers:
for they shall be called the children of God.
MATTHEW 5:9 KJV

A four-year-old said to his mother,
"It must be bedtime because you're very crabby."

The Bible talks about making peace. It is an action. It is proactive. Some churches have a ceremony in which they give peace. People turn to each other and say, "Peace be unto you," the reply being, "And also to you." It is a blessing and refreshing ceremony and can spread quickly. Try it with your neighbors and with people you meet in everyday life. Don't try to force it into the conversation. Use it as a parting blessing. Instead of saying, "Have a nice day" try, "Peace be unto you." A local church challenged its members to do this. They were surprised at how people responded. Instead of thinking the "blessers" were crazy, almost every "blessee" said thank you. It seemed like it had made their day. God has graciously given us His peace. It is up to us to share that peace with others. Who do we know that we can give peace to? Our families, our friends, and any strangers we meet. Many people pray for world peace but what are they doing to help it come about? Let us be peacemakers so everyone will know we are the children of God.

The children of God share the peace of God.

Needing Help

My help comes from the LORD, who made heaven and earth.
PSALM 121:2 NKJV

A five-year-old boy had a nightmare.
When his mother went into his room to soothe him
and make sure he was all right, the boy said,
"I don't want you. I want Daddy. You can't beat up the bad guys!"

When we're scared, we want a superhero to come and rescue us. But just like a nightmare isn't real, our fears, though extremely scary, aren't real. We dread things that haven't even happened yet. God, the ultimate superhero, can give us peace despite our scary circumstances. We look back on the story of Esther and think, "Good for her!" But let's go live the story of Esther. Although we know how it turned out for this Jewish queen, Esther didn't know what was going to happen when she was going through it. She was in actual fear for her life. If the king had not held out his scepter to her, she would have been killed. We, too, can live through some scary circumstances. And our fear comes from not knowing how they will turn out. But peace comes from realizing that God knows how everything will turn out, and that no matter what happens, it is all part of His plan to bring us good. Let's follow the example of Esther who, although fearful, did the right thing. And God brought great good from her act of obedience.

All our dependence is on God and
all our "expectation is from Him" (Psalm 62:5 NKJV).

"This Is the Way"

*Whether you turn to the right or to the left,
your ears will hear a voice behind you, saying,
"This is the way; walk in it."*
ISAIAH 30:21 NIV

*A seven-year-old girl was fascinated
with her mother's turn signal in the car.
"Mama," she said in awe, "how does that little arrow know
which way we are going to turn?"*

God is our true guide. When we are confused about which way to go, we can ask Him to show us. He literally guides our steps and shows us one step at a time how we are to proceed. With God directing us, we can confidently follow the path He has set before us. Jesus told His disciples that He is the way (see John 14:6). So when we walk in the way, we are walking with Jesus. As long as our eyes are on Him, our steps will not falter. We will not fall down or be left behind. We teach our toddlers to walk by crouching down in front of them with our arms outstretched and encouraging them to come to us. Picture God doing that with us—stooping down in front of us with His arms open wide, urging us to come to Him. We can walk our Christian walk with peace and confidence knowing that God is always with us and around us. All we need to do is open our ears to His voice and our eyes to His path.

The best way to go is God's way.

"WHAT WILL YOU DO?"

*"So do not worry or be anxious about tomorrow,
for tomorrow will have worries and anxieties of its own.
Sufficient for each day is its own trouble."*
MATTHEW 6:34 AMP

*An eight-year-old girl asked her mother,
"What will you do when your car runs out of miles?"*

The bills were all overdue. The mortgage payment was late. The groceries were getting scarce. The car had two bald tires. The roof had started leaking and that morning she had gotten a run in her last pair of pantyhose. Carole sat down on her sofa, put her head in her hands, and felt like she was ready to cry. But instead she prayed softly, "Thank You, Father, for all I have, for all You have given me. You see my situation. You know my needs. You have always provided for me in the past, and I know You will provide for me now because You promised that You would." With a renewed sense of peace, Carole got ready to leave for work. Her circumstances were still the same, but Carole was in touch with the one above all circumstances. She trusted God to work everything out. Try this exercise: Can you remember what you were worried about five years ago? Maybe you can't. But if you can, remember that God brought you through that, and He didn't bring you this far to abandon you now. He has promised to provide and to work everything out. And God always keeps His promises. Peace comes from trusting in Him.

God is not our last resort—He is our primary Source.

Yelling at Fear

Yea, though I walk through the valley of the shadow of death,
I will fear no evil; for You are with me.
PSALM 23:4 NKJV

A three-year-old boy was afraid of the family cat.
One day his father heard the boy yelling
from behind his closed bedroom door,
"The cat has a stupid face!"

We seem to be most afraid of what we think might happen. Note that the writer of Psalm 23:4 is not afraid of death itself, just its shadow. But yelling at what we're afraid of won't make it go away. Nor will fussing, fretting, fuming, worrying, losing sleep, and stressing ourselves out. Those things won't change our situation one bit. On the other hand, we *can* simply trust God. Although doing so still won't change our situation, it will change us. When we trust in God and give Him our fears, He will give us His peace in return. Just like a river flows in, around, and through the obstacles in its way, God's peace can flow in, around, and through us as we face the obstacles of our lives here on this earth. God knows us. He knows what scares us. He tells us that His perfect love casts out our fear, because "fear involves torment" (1 John 4:18 NKJV). Most of us know what it's like to be tormented by fear. But God will deliver us from our terrors—if we just let Him.

The reverent fear of the Lord will
keep us from fearing the things of this world.

A Light Spoon

The LORD will give strength to His people;
the LORD will bless His people with peace.
PSALM 29:11 NKJV

A three-year-old boy was singing the song, "A Spoonful of Sugar."
When he got to the end of the chorus, he sang,
"And your spoon is light today
[In a most delightful way]."

Thanks to God, our spoons can be light. Some days, when our worries weigh heavily upon us, we may feel like we're trying to dig our way out of all the difficulties that surround us. But God gives us the strength to go on. And when we are operating in His strength, He gives us the blessing of His peace. He understands that we're human and frail as dust. After all, He created us. And He understands that we worry. So He, who has tender compassion for us, instructs us to cast all our cares upon Him (see Psalm 55:22; 1 Peter 5:7). The word *cast* has the meaning of continual action—we are to cast and to keep on casting our cares upon Him. While we are casting our cares away, He replaces our concerns with His peace "in a most delightful way." God's spoonful of sugar is the constant blessing of His peace. This is the sweetness He adds to our lives to make them not just bearable but delightful.

With God, life is sweet indeed!

PRAYING

Asking for Inappropriate Things

When you ask, you do not receive,
because you ask with wrong motives,
that you may spend what you get on your pleasures.
JAMES 4:3 NIV

A four-year-old boy said to his mother,
"Mom, you should buy me a credit card for my birthday."

Although nothing is impossible with God, sometimes we ask Him for things that are not appropriate for us. Our children sometimes ask us for inappropriate things, such as a credit card or permission to drive the family car before they get their license. We say no because we know what is best for them. In the same way, Father God says no to the inappropriate requests of His children. He knows that we don't really need to win the lottery or own our own 747 jet plane. He could give us these things if He chose to do so, but He loves us too much to allow our flights of fancy to become reality. God doesn't want us to have anything that will take our focus off Him. Money or possessions may actually interfere with our relationship with God, especially if we pay more attention to them than we do to our prayer life. Instead of wishing for great wealth or massive possessions, we need to pray for the right things—love for our neighbors, salvation for the lost, intercession for the ill. Our powerful prayers shouldn't be wasted on pleas for pleasures.

Prayer is not a magic formula to get what we want;
it is a way for God to show His powerful love for us.

BANJO KAZOOIE

Find your delight in the Lord.
Then he will give you everything your heart really wants.
PSALM 37:4 NIrV

Right before Christmas, a six-year-old boy
was saying grace at the dinner table.
He said, "Dear God, thank You for God
and for the Banjo Kazooie that I really,
really want bad and Santa Claus can bring it to me
for Christmas and the food. In Jesus' name, amen."

In his prayer, this six-year-old boy did something that we are always supposed to do—he thanked God for the Banjo Kazooie even though he hadn't gotten it yet. Most times, we thank God after He has graciously granted one of our requests. But the Bible is full of examples and instructions that say we are to thank God for His blessings before we ever receive them (see John 6:11; 11:41). He delights in us when we show this kind of trust in Him (see Psalm 149:4). Psalm 37:4 also instructs us to find our delight in Him. When we do, something wonderful happens: He puts His will and His plan in our hearts. So when we pray for our heart's desire, our petition is for His will and His plan. If we love God passionately, if we want to please, obey, and honor Him, then His plan automatically becomes our desire.

When our delight is in the Lord, our hearts truly desire Him.

"Make 'Em Hurry"

*Jesus answered, "It is written: 'Man does not live on bread alone,
but on every word that comes from the mouth of God.'"*
MATTHEW 4:4 NIV

*Asked to say the blessing at the dinner table,
a six-year-old girl said,
"Make 'em hurry, Lord. I'm hungry."*

We're not just in a hurry at the dinner table. We seem to be in a hurry all the time. We want immediate answers to our prayers. But many times we have to wait. Why? Because God takes time to not only prepare the answer to our prayers but to prepare us to receive it. For hundreds of years, the Israelites prayed for the Messiah to come. The whole time they were praying, God was preparing them and the rest of the world for Jesus Christ's coming. Then the early Christians prayed earnestly for Jesus to return. Two thousand years later, we are still watching and praying for that event. Meanwhile, God is preparing us and the rest of the world for Jesus' return. Effective prayer is not directive. God doesn't need our counsel on how to get things done. Instead He uses our prayers to teach us many things about His timing and His method. The Bible tells us how He answered the prayers of many of His people, revealing that God is very creative. He doesn't respond to our prayers in the way we expect. That's because God's answer is always better than anything we can imagine.

*Before the answer comes our way,
our souls are changed when we pray.*

CAREFUL WHAT YOU ASK FOR

Ask, and it shall be given you.
MATTHEW 7:7 KJV

A three-year-old overheard his mother telling someone
that everyone had chicken pox except him.
That night when he said his prayers,
the little boy asked God to
please give him the chicken pox.

Sometimes we may interpret Matthew 7:7 to mean that whatever we ask God for, we will get. But Jesus just said, "Ask, and it shall be given." He didn't say *what* would be given. If we ask God for something and trust His will, then what we receive will be His best for us. It might not be exactly what we think we asked for, nor what we think is best, but it will be what our Father *knows* is best. There is an old saying—"Be careful what you ask for." Very good advice. Sometimes we ask God for things that we shouldn't have. But God knows exactly what we need. Matthew 7:7 isn't a magic wand we wave to get God to give us everything we want. It is an admonition that we should be careful what we ask for. Psalm 145:18-19 says, the Lord is near to "all who call upon Him in truth. He will fulfill the desire of those who fear Him" (NKJV). God knows the true desires of our hearts better than we ever could.

God has His best things for the few
Who dare to stand the test.
He has His second best for those
Who will not have His best.

"Dear God, Please"

We do not know what we ought to pray for,
but the Spirit himself intercedes for us through wordless groans.
ROMANS 8:26 NIV

A three-year-old boy asked if he could say grace at the dinner table.
He said, "Dear God, please, please, please, please, please. Amen."

God gave us the privilege of prayer because He wants to hear from us. He wants to have conversations with us. How wonderful to know that even when we cannot properly express our thoughts, feelings, or wishes, God knows exactly what we're trying to say. When our hearts are too anguished or overwhelmed for us to express ourselves coherently, the Holy Spirit gently and kindly interprets our prayers for us. Because He is with us 24-7, He knows us better than we know ourselves. Being able to be in constant contact with the Creator of all things is a powerful aid to our peace of mind. Prayer is the fastest means we have of communication. It is as fast as a thought. And just as fast comes God's comfort to us. Prayer not only puts us in touch with God but it also allows God to touch our lives. Nothing is too great or small to tell God. He loves us and pities us and helps us. We can truly cast all our cares upon Him because not only does He care for us, but He knows what's best for us and can give us exactly what we need whether it be comfort, encouragement, wisdom, or anything else.

God is waiting to hear from you. Give Him a shout-out today!

EXPECTATIONS

And it shall come to pass, that before they call,
I will answer; and while they are yet speaking, I will hear.
ISAIAH 65:24 KJV

A five-year-old boy came home from school all dejected.
Knowing that his class had gone to the bakery on a field trip,
his mother was surprised that he wasn't happy.
"Didn't you go to the bakery?" she asked.
"Yes," the boy replied. "And we got a cookie."
"So why aren't you happy?" his mother asked.
"The teacher said we were going on a field trip,"
the boy replied, "but we didn't see a field."

Sometimes God's answer to our prayer is cookies instead of fields. But we are so focused on what we are praying for specifically that we miss His greater blessing. In Acts 12, Peter was in jail. The disciples were all gathered at the house of Mary (John's mom), praying for Peter's release. Meanwhile, God sent an angel to get Peter out of jail. When Peter arrived at Mary's house, he knocked on the door. A girl named Rhoda went to answer. But when she heard Peter's voice, instead of opening the door, she ran back in and excitedly told the disciples that Peter was at the door. Because they didn't believe her, they kept on praying. So Peter stood and knocked at the door until someone finally answered it. Then there was great rejoicing. Are we still praying while God's answer to our prayer is already knocking at the door of our heart? We mustn't let our expectations make us blind to God's answers.

When we pray with faith and pray with hope,
we can expect great answers from God.

"God Bless the Q-Tip"

*The earnest (heartfelt, continued) prayer of a righteous man
makes tremendous power available [dynamic in its working].*
JAMES 5:16 AMP

*A four-year-old girl who didn't like going to bed would stretch out
her nighttime prayers as long as she could.
Her mother would watch as the girl would open one eye
and look around to see things that she could include in her prayer.
One night the child was praying, "God bless my bed. God bless my dolls.
God bless my shoes." Suddenly, to her mother's surprise,
the child said, "God bless the Q-tip."
The mother looked and sure enough there was a Q-tip lying
on the floor near where the girl was kneeling.*

Sometimes we may be guilty of using prayer for reasons other than God intended, such as for staying up or impressing someone. But because prayer is a powerful, God-given tool, we must be careful to pray with meaning. There was once a poor widow woman who, by all evidence, loved the Lord and had a close relationship with Him. In her community and church, she was known as a woman of prayer. People from all walks of life would come to her and ask her to pray for them. Her prayers were blessings, not only for the person she was praying for but for anyone else who was listening. No one ever complained about how long her prayers were; they were only aware of how vital and intense her petitions and praise were. She knew how to pray effectively.

Heartfelt prayers have tremendous power.

Knowing What We're Saying

Blessed be the Lord, the God of Israel, forever and ever! And all the people said Amen! and praised the Lord.
1 CHRONICLES 16:36 AMP

When asked by his Sunday school teacher if he knew what amen meant, a four-year-old boy said, "Th-th-th-th-that's all folks!"

The word *amen* actually means "so be it." So, when we end our prayers with "In Jesus' name, amen," we are actually saying, "If this is Your will for us according to Jesus, then so be it." But we need to know more than just what the word *amen* means. We need to concentrate on what our prayers are actually saying. The Lord's Prayer (see Matthew 6:9–13) is not just some prayer formula Jesus gave to His disciples. It is an actual prayer to God. We don't want to recite the Lord's Prayer without really thinking about what we are saying. Many times in the psalms the word *Selah* appears. This word means to pause and reflect on what has just been said. When we are praying, we need to pause and reflect on what we are saying. We need to speak with God in faith and earnestly from our hearts, making sure the things we are asking for are according to His will. When we do so, He answers us with things greater and more glorious than we had imagined.

Prayer is a privilege, not an obligation.

Many Words

"And when you pray, do not use vain repetitions as the heathen do.
For they think that they will be heard for their many words."
MATTHEW 6:7 NKJV

A three-year-old boy was praying in his Sunday school class.
His prayer rambled on and on.
One of his classmates mumbled something.
The three-year-old stopped and said, "I already prayed for that."
Then he continued on with his prayer.

There are people in this world who seem to believe that the longer you pray the better your prayer. Some people think the hymn called "Sweet Hour of Prayer" implies that we should pray for an hour at a time. But prayer is not supposed to be an onerous duty. Nor is it something to be checked off our to-do list. Prayer, our method of communicating with God, is a privilege. We can tell Him anything and everything, day or night. But we don't have to drone on and on just to prove we are spiritual. We can shoot out one-second prayers—such as "God. . .help!"—or twenty-minute prayers. How long we speak does not matter to God but what we say does. We need to engage our hearts, not just our tongues. And while God is always ready and willing to listen to us, effective prayer means that we, in turn, listen to Him. Prayer is a dialogue, not a monologue. We get to meet with God and He with us. That makes prayer sweet indeed.

God is not impressed with our many words
but with the intention of our hearts.

Perspective

*Now godliness with contentment is great gain. For we brought
nothing into this world, and it is certain we can carry nothing out.
And having food and clothing, with these we shall be content.*

1 TIMOTHY 6:6–8 NKJV

*An eight-year-old boy was watching his mother dish out ice cream.
Eying the bowl, he said, "All that for Grandpa?"
"No, son," said his mother, "this one is for you."
The boy said, "Oh, what a little bit."*

There is a saying: The other guy's grass is always greener. If
we look around at what others have, we might run the risk
of becoming discontent with what we have. According to
the verses above, if we have food and clothing, we should be
content. Unfortunately, too often, we find ourselves envying
what someone else has. We are jealous of the lottery winner or
our friend whose business is booming or our neighbor's new car.
Looking around can get us in trouble. Looking up will always
save us. When we look to our Father from whom all blessings
flow, we no longer are concerned with what others have. We
are too busy praising Him for all the things He has given us.
God is so good to us. Statistically, the poorest person in our
neighborhood is still wealthier than 90 percent of the world's
population.

God desires that we be content with what we have.

Recognizing the Answer

*Call unto me, and I will answer thee, and show thee great
and mighty things, which thou knowest not.*
JEREMIAH 33:3 KJV

*A seven-year-old girl asked her mother, "How do you spell TV?"
Her mother replied, "T-V."
"I know," said the girl, "but how do you spell it?"*

Certain things in the Bible are absolutely clear. Yet sometimes
we can't seem to grasp the obvious. We are focused on our own
idea and don't recognize the answer. That is what happened
when Jesus appeared as the Messiah. Although the Bible was
very clear about how He would come and when He would come,
the prevailing idea of the day was that the Messiah would be an
earthly king who would overthrow Rome and restore Israel to
glory. But there was at least one person who recognized the
Messiah—even when He was in the form of a tiny baby. God
had promised Simeon that he would see the Messiah before he
died. After the days of Mary's purification, Joseph and Mary
brought Baby Jesus to the temple to present Him to the Lord.
When Simeon saw the Baby, he took Him into his arms and
blessed God saying, "Lord, now You are letting Your servant
depart in peace, according to Your word; for my eyes have seen
Your salvation" (Luke 2:29-30 NKJV). Simeon could see God's
answer to his prayer in this little Baby. Indeed, all the answers to
all our prayers are in Jesus.

God comes not to answer prayer but as the answer to prayer.

"Shut Up! I'm Praying!"

Lord, even before I speak a word, you know all about it.
PSALM 139:4 NIrV

Eager to recite the new grace he had learned at preschool,
a four-year-old boy started singing the little song.
When his two-year-old brother joined in,
the four-year-old stopped and said, "Shut up! I'm praying!"

We might laugh at this four-year-old's reaction, but we must be careful that we don't have that attitude when we pray. Prayer isn't about what we are saying but about the intent of our hearts. Some people think of prayer as a thing in and of itself. They are more concerned with their phrasing and the way it sounds than they are actually talking to God. Perhaps they are giving a prayer in church or in front of some group and they are concerned with what people will think of how they pray. But prayer isn't about impressing other people. When he was on Mount Carmel with the prophets of Baal, Elijah prayed that God would send the fire he asked for so that the people would know that God was God and that Elijah was his servant (see 1 Kings 18:20–39). Elijah's prayer was answered because he prayed for the right thing. He wasn't praying for God to send fire so that people would be impressed with him but so that they would be impressed with God. God not only hears every word we say, He knows what we're going to say. He knows the intent of our hearts.

God longs to have a heart-to-heart conversation with us.

Timing

There's a time for everything that is done on earth.
ECCLESIASTES 3:1 NIrV

"I want juice," a two-year-old boy announced.
"And what is the magic word?" his nanny prompted him.
"Now," he replied.

Often Christians seem to think that *now* is the magic word. Part of being mature is the ability to understand that timing is everything. And God's timing is perfect. Sometimes, while waiting for something, we receive the insight that what we asked for isn't really what we want after all. Other times while waiting, we can receive an added fillip of anticipation. If everything everyone wanted came about immediately, there would be chaos. On the same day a farmer prays for rain, a bride may be praying for a beautiful sunny day. "God is not the author of confusion" (1 Corinthians 14:33 KJV). He not only knows what we need, He knows when we need it. We can rely on His timing. When the Israelites were crying out to God to be delivered from their slavery in Egypt, God answered them in His own good time. By the time Pharaoh was ready to let the Israelites leave, the Egyptians were so eager to get rid of them that they gave the Jews all manner of treasures to take with them. Basically the Egyptians were trying to bribe the Israelites to leave. So the Jews departed with many more material goods than they would have had if they had left Egypt the first time Moses spoke with Pharaoh.

**God answers our prayers in His time and
more amazingly than we could have imagined.**

STEWARDSHIP

ANY EXCUSE

*Be doers of the Word [obey the message],
and not merely listeners to it.*
JAMES 1:22 AMP

*A mother came upon her ten-year-old son just as he cut
a hunk of hair off the center of the top of his head.
"What are you doing?" the mother demanded.
"Cutting my hair," the boy replied. "It was in my eyes."*

We can think of a million excuses to do or not do anything. But James says that to do the will of God, we must actually *do* it. The word *do* implies action. We can't just sit around thinking about doing what God wants us to do, nor can we just say we're going to do it. We have to actually get up and take action. On the other hand, we shouldn't try to prevent others from doing what they know God wants them to do. There was a woman who resented all the people in her church who went to visit the sick at the hospital. She didn't want to go herself and thought that others going made her look bad. But if we are followers of Christ, we can't be concerned with what others think. We are only bound by what God thinks. The Creator of the universe gave us our lives here with a purpose—to glorify and honor Him. Doing what He wills us to do is the only way to accomplish that purpose—no excuses allowed.

Our excuses are ludicrous to the God who sees all and knows all.

FOLLOW THE LEADER

Follow my example, just as I follow the example of Christ.
1 CORINTHIANS 11:1 NIrV

*A father asked his four-year-old son why
the son was always the leader when they played
follow-the-leader. His son replied,
"When I was born, they told me I was the leader
and all the other children would follow me."*

This boy isn't really wrong. Leadership is one of the gifts God gives to certain people. It is an awesome responsibility and God expects us to use it wisely. To be good leaders, we must be sure we are leading our followers in the right direction—and that means leading them to the Lord. The way we do this is by getting to know God personally, learning to understand His activity in our lives, and expressing His love to others. God says that if we trust Him, He will direct our paths (see Proverbs 3:5–6). To lead, we have to follow. We follow where God leads us and as we do, the ones following us go in the same direction. Even if we're not the designated leader, other people watch us. As Christians we are under constant scrutiny by the world. We need to make sure that what others see in us points them to God.

*We are God's hand extended
Reaching out to those distressed
To lift them up and lead them on
And share as we've been blessed.*

Grocery List

Pray without ceasing.
1 THESSALONIANS 5:17 KJV

*"What are you doing?" a five-year-old girl asked her mother.
"Making a grocery list," her mother replied.
"Well, you need to put some food on there," the girl said,
"because we're out of food."*

We know that we are to be good stewards of all God has given us. We should also be good stewards with the privilege of our prayers. Instead of praying generically, saying things like, "God bless the missionaries," or "God bless the sick and poor people," we need to pray specifically. What missionaries do we know about? Let's pray for them by name. When we pray for the people we know who are ill, let's hold them up individually to the Lord, presenting them and their specific needs to Him. We can make our prayers even more powerful and meaningful if we pray with others—even just one other person. Jesus said that where two or three are gathered together in His name, He is in the midst of them (see Matthew 18:20). Prayer is not just something we should mumble in the morning when we get up or at night before we go to sleep. It is a gift from God, something we can use for His honor and glory. Just like we are good stewards of our time, our finances, and the material blessings God gives us, we need to be good stewards with our prayers.

**The more specifically we pray that God's will be done,
the more powerful our prayers.**

Happy When They Share

Whoever has this world's goods, and sees his brother in need, and shuts up his heart from him, how does the love of God abide in him?
1 JOHN 3:17 NKJV

During Sunday school, a five-year-old boy learned a song about sharing. At home, he tried to get his three-year-old brother to give him a certain toy. When the brother refused to give it up, the five-year-old sang the sharing song. When he finished the song, the older brother said, "See? Kids are happy when they share." And then he snatched the toy out of his little brother's hand.

As Christians we're supposed to share. Jesus told the early believers that if someone sued them for their shirt, they were to give the person their coat (see Matthew 5:40). Sharing is one of the things that shows others we are children of God. Coveting, which is the opposite of sharing, is not just admiring what someone else has—it is envying them for having it and making ourselves miserable wanting it. God knows that coveting will make us discontented and sharing will make us happy. And when you really think about it, there's actually no such thing as personal possessions. All we have is from God and belongs to Him. He wants us to share these blessings with others. That's why He gave them to us. When we seek God first, we find that He has already provided all we need. And He's given us plenty to share.

We don't need to covet the blessings of another
But share what we have with one another.

Not Important

*"But seek first the kingdom of God and His righteousness,
and all these things shall be added to you."*
MATTHEW 6:33 NKJV

*A twelve-year-old girl wrote a letter to her aunt.
"I'm writing you from school. Don't worry.
It's not an important class."*

We don't always know what's important. George Mueller (1805–1898) was a man of prayer who trusted God to supply all he needed. He and his wife had started an orphanage in England. One morning the children were all sitting at the breakfast table even though there was nothing to eat. As they gave thanks, a baker knocked on the door with bread for everyone. Apparently he couldn't sleep the night before. He'd had a "feeling" the Lord wanted him to bake bread for the orphans! What if that baker hadn't heeded God's prompting? While making his bread, this baker might not have known that he was being an answer to someone's prayer, but he certainly found out the next day—to the joy of many souls! We, too, might know that we are the answer to someone's prayer. That's why it is so important for us to do what God tells us to do. Only He sees the big picture. We are an integral part of God's universe. What we do matters to God and to others. It's not up to us to decide if something is important enough to do or not. If it weren't important, He wouldn't have asked us to do it.

Everything we do for God is important.

Reflecting Jesus' Light

*Let your light so shine before men that they may see your
moral excellence and your praiseworthy, noble,
and good deeds and recognize and honor and praise
and glorify your Father Who is in heaven.*
MATTHEW 5:16 AMP

*"I need a new light bulb," a six-year-old girl told her father.
"My light bulb is out of light."*

Jesus said we are to let our light shine. How do we do that? By the way we live. In Acts 1:8 Jesus told the disciples that when the Holy Spirit came upon them, they would *be* witnesses; their whole lives would witness to the goodness of God. We reflect Jesus' light in many ways—neighborliness, generosity, hospitality, our work ethic, and perhaps most of all in our faith and hope in God when we are going through difficult times. It is important to tell people our testimony so they can see how God works and what He's done and take courage when they are in difficult situations. Being a Christian is much more than just announcing it to the world. It is a way of life. It is seeing ourselves through God's eyes. It is doing His will with His strength. God has a spiritual purpose for all He asks us to do. The main purpose is shining our light so others will see what we do and glorify God.

We are here to reflect the light of Jesus into a dark world.

Taking Care of Business

But we urge you, brethren, that you increase more and more;
that you also aspire to lead a quiet life, to mind your own business,
and to work with your own hands, as we commanded you.
1 THESSALONIANS 4:10–11 NKJV

A nine-year-old girl was quite annoyed with her teacher.
The teacher had told the girl's sister something
the nine-year-old had done.
"This is my business," the girl told her teacher.
"Why are you telling her? I can take care of my own business."

The Bible actually tells us to mind our own business. This is good advice. When we are busy doing what we're supposed to be doing, we don't have time to look around and try to figure out what someone else should be doing. God created each one of us to fulfill a specific purpose in His kingdom. Just like every cell in our bodies is filled with one purpose—our well-being—so we are cells in the body of Christ and our purpose is to see to the well-being of the whole Body. We do that by minding the business God gave us to mind and not poking our nose into everyone else's affairs. God doesn't overwhelm us with things to do. He gives us one task at a time. When we complete that, He gives us the next thing to do. Now that's taking care of business!

If we are focused on our own business,
we don't have time to mind anyone else's.

Knowing Who We Are

*We all, who with unveiled faces contemplate the Lord's glory,
are being transformed into his image with ever-increasing glory,
which comes from the Lord, who is the Spirit.*
2 Corinthians 3:18 NIV

*A nanny came into the living room to find her four-year-old
charge sitting dejectedly on the sofa. "Are you bored?" she asked him.
"No," he replied with a sigh, "I'm Paul."*

When Moses came down from Mount Sinai, where he'd been in the presence of the Lord, he didn't know that the skin on his face was shining. The Israelites saw him and were afraid because darkness cannot stand the light. So, after speaking to them, he covered his face (see Exodus 34:29–35). As believers, we are in the process of becoming more and more like Jesus. The closer we get to His light, the more we shine. Jesus is the Light of the world. We are a reflection of that light—so we need to shine as brightly as we can. The more we know who Jesus truly is, the more we know who we are and why God put us here on this earth. Our light may make some people uncomfortable. They may ask us to block our shine from them. But God didn't put us here to hide His light. We are to be reflectors of Jesus, Who is the Light of the world. As God has said, "Let there be light" (Genesis 1:3).

We are privileged that God uses us to glorify Himself.

USING WHAT GOD GIVES US

*And truly Jesus did many other signs in the presence of His disciples,
which are not written in this book; but these are written that you
may believe that Jesus is the Christ, the Son of God, and that
believing you may have life in His name.*
JOHN 20:30–31 NKJV

*An eight-year-old girl was drawing a picture of a birthday cake for
her grandmother's birthday. As she drew a rectangle for the cake itself,
she looked at her grandmother and said,
"Wait a minute." Then she turned the paper over and drew a much
bigger rectangle. "I need more room for all those candles," she explained.*

We may think we need more room sometimes. Perhaps our
house is crowded or perhaps we would like a bigger office at
work. But we can bloom where we are planted no matter how
cramped we think our garden is. In Jesus' day, the Pharisees were
always taunting Him to show them signs to prove who He was.
But because Jesus didn't have to prove Himself, He didn't. After
every sign and miracle that Jesus did, the people praised God.
The Son took no praise or glory for Himself although He could
have. His signs glorified God and made believers out of the
people. We don't need to ask for more. After all, He has already
given us everything we need. And He has shown us by His life
how to use our blessings to glorify our Father in heaven.

Good stewards work with what they have.

Putting On the Dog

*A mother was watching a video of her cousin's wedding.
As she watched the elaborate proceedings, she commented,
"Boy, they really put on the dog."
Her eleven-year-old daughter came over to see the video.
"They got a dog, too?" she asked. "Where is it?"*

God is very explicit in the Bible about how poor people are to be treated. Most of us have the opportunity to share our material blessings with those less fortunate. But we are obligated to do so with the right attitude. In Jesus' day, certain prominent men in the city would have a servant go before them, blowing a trumpet as they "graciously" bestowed money on the poor. These men wanted to be sure that everyone knew they were being generous. If all our giving is simply so that people can praise us and give us Woman of the Year awards, then Jesus says that's all the reward we'll ever get. But if we share our material blessings in secret, with the attitude that everything comes from God and we are just His stewards, then God Himself will reward us—not just here on earth but later, as well.

God's rewards surpass man's praise.

"Nana's Cobweb"

Christ also loved the church and gave Himself for her. . .
that He might present her to Himself a glorious church,
not having spot or wrinkle or any such thing,
but that she should be holy and without blemish.
EPHESIANS 5:25, 27 NKJV

A woman was having a party at her house
while her four-year-old granddaughter was visiting.
As the guests arrived, the little girl would take them into the
dining room to show them something she thought was wonderful.
At first the woman thought her granddaughter
was showing the guests the buffet.
Then she heard her granddaughter say to some guests
"Look! "It's Nana's cobweb!"
The grandmother went into the dining room, and sure enough,
there was a cobweb dangling from the chandelier.

We may be mortified to have our flaws pointed out to others. But where I see a cobweb, someone else may see a thing of beauty. Beauty truly is in the eye of the beholder. And who beholds us? God. He sees us as the spotless Bride of Christ—not a pockmarked sinner. Our Creator God wants us to be at peace with who He crafted us to be. Although it is very healthy to be aware that we might have a problem to correct, it is extremely unhealthy to see ourselves as only substandard beings. When we perceive ourselves as God sees us, we can be better stewards of the lives He has blessed us with.

We need to look at ourselves through God's eyes.

TRUSTING

Perfect in His Sight

As for God, His way is perfect; the word of the LORD is proven.
2 SAMUEL 22:31 NKJV

A grandmother said to her five-year-old grandson,
"God made you so handsome."
The boy replied, "And He gave you an old face."

Maybe we think that someone else got a better deal than we did. But God's blessings are individual and perfect for us. Ruth may have thought that she had been cheated in life. Her husband died and her mother-in-law was moving back to Bethlehem. Because Ruth considered Naomi to be her family, she accompanied her to Bethlehem. When they arrived, they had nothing, so Ruth gleaned in the fields to get enough grain for them to eat. While Ruth was gleaning, Naomi's kinsman, Boaz, noticed the young widow. Boaz loved Ruth and married her. They had a son, Obed. Obed had a son, Jesse, and Jesse had a son, David. Ruth went from being a poor widow to being the great-grandmother of the greatest king Israel ever had—David. And Ruth became one of only five women mentioned in the genealogy of Jesus (see Matthew 1:5). Ruth was an ancestor of the King of kings. But she didn't know any of this was going to happen when she went to Bethlehem with Naomi. Only God knows what He has in store for us. We can safely trust Him with our present and our future.

What we think is a raw deal now might be
the greatest blessing of our lives.

BEING AFRAID

*Fear not [there is nothing to fear], for I am with you; do not look
around you in terror and be dismayed, for I am your God.
I will strengthen and harden you to difficulties, yes, I will help you;
yes, I will hold you up and retain you with
My [victorious] right hand of rightness and justice.*
ISAIAH 41:10 AMP

*A three-year-old girl awoke from her nap and ran to her nanny.
"I had a bad dream," the girl said. "It scared the wrinkles out of me."*

All our fears are really just bad dreams. The antidote to being
afraid is to trust God. The Bible is full of stories about how
God delivered His people from out of their dire circumstances.
Reading these accounts can give us some perspective on our
own troubles. Is our current quandary as bad as being in a whale
for three days like Jonah? Does it compare with Paul and Silas
who were beaten and jailed? Are we facing beasts as fierce
as those with Daniel in the lions' den? Would we trade what
we're going through for Elijah's situation as he hid in a cave
because Jezebel was trying to kill him? Even though our current
experience may be serious and scary, it can't compare to that
of the first Christians who were being killed for their beliefs.
Every one of those people trusted God to save them, and He
delivered them all.

**No matter how bad we may think we have it,
God will get us through.**

CARRY YOU

*Even to your old age I am He, and even to hair white
with age will I carry you. I have made,
and I will bear; yes, I will carry and will save you.*
ISAIAH 46:4 AMP

*A three-year-old boy was walking with his mother.
Raising his arm, he said to her, "Carry my hand."*

God carries more than our hand. He carries our entire being—mind, body, spirit, and soul. Isaiah 46:4 is the greatest retirement benefit a believer can have. God doesn't abandon us when we get old. In fact, the older we get and the more we trust Him, the more He carries us. God promises to take care of us all our lives and that we will one day live with Him in eternity. And God always keeps His promises. Trust is like a circle. The more we trust God, the more He proves Himself to us; and the more God proves Himself to us, the more we trust Him. We trust Him when He says that He will work all things out for our good and that He can redeem any situation we may find ourselves in. Since God has taken care of us our whole lives, we trust Him enough to know that He's not going to stop now. No matter what comes our way, we can count on Him to take care of us each and every day.

*Father God carries us through thick and thin—
through all our todays and tomorrows.*

"Don't Be Scary"

The angel said to her, "Do not be afraid, Mary.
God is very pleased with you."
LUKE 1:30 NIrV

When asked, "What special thing did the angel say to Mary?"
a three-year-old boy replied, "Don't be scary."

Through the "valley of the shadow" (Psalm 23:4 NKJV), the Shepherd leads us. We try not to look around at the scary darkness. We try not to wonder what might be coming out of the shadows toward us. We stay focused on our Shepherd. He is the light to our path. He is the way to our goal. His love surrounds us on all sides. So no matter what may come, we are completely sheltered in God, the rock of our salvation. We don't have to be "scary." All we have to do is follow as our Shepherd leads us to green pastures and still waters. Being in the valley can be frightening. But the God of the mountain is the God of the valley. The God of the day is the God of the night. He goes before us in a pillar of cloud that leads us, and stays behind us in a pillar of fire that protects us (see Exodus 13:21–22). We don't need an angel to tell us not to be afraid. We have God Himself telling us to trust in Him and He will take care of us.

We don't have to be afraid. God is very pleased
with each one of us.

"Grandma's Dog"

*"Whoever does not receive the kingdom of God
like a child will not enter it at all."*
MARK 10:15 NASB

*A mother had the unpleasant task of informing her children that
their grandmother's dog, whom they loved, had died.
As they were in the car going to their grandmother's house,
the mother noticed that her five-year-old daughter was whispering to
herself in the backseat. "What are you doing?" the mother asked.
The daughter replied, "I'm asking God to make Grandma's dog
all better and send her back down here to us."*

One of the reasons God gave us children is so that we can learn from them. Our children have a complete trust in God that should be inspirational to us. They believe God can and will do anything. We should have this type of trust in God. Jesus said that if we ask anything of the Father that is in accordance with His will, we shall have it (see John 14:13; 1 John 3:22). Learning to trust God more helps us to know Him more. The more we know Him, the more we know what His will is for us. Then we pray asking for things we know He wills us to have and we trust Him to give them to us. With a child's absolute faith, we trust in Abba God. By doing so, we gain access to His awesome kingdom.

With childlike trust, believe!

He's Always There

She called the name of the LORD that spake unto her,
Thou God seest me.
GENESIS 16:13 KJV

A three-year-old girl was noisy during a church service.
"Hush," her mother told her.
"This is God's house and you need to be quiet."
"Why?" asked the child. "He's never home."

Fortunately for us, God is always "home." But sometimes maybe we behave as if God isn't all-present, all-seeing, and all-knowing. Maybe we feel like He isn't really watching us right this very moment. Hagar was running from Sarah who had been unkind to her. She ended up near a fountain of water in the desert and the Angel of the Lord found her there. The Angel told Hagar to return and submit to Sarah. He also told her that her son would be the father of many nations. Hagar was amazed that the Lord cared enough about her to come find her. And that is why she called Him the "God Who Sees Me." How comforting to know that our loving God sees us. He finds us wherever we are—in whatever wilderness we are wandering. He has clear directions for us, as well as blessings. Knowing that God loves us causes our spirits to soar, our souls to sing, and our hearts to overflow with adoration of Him. It makes it that much easier for us to trust Him when He says He will take care of us today, tomorrow, and every day.

God has a special place in His heart for us.

"I Didn't Ask You"

Then I heard a loud voice saying in heaven, "Now salvation, and strength, and the kingdom of our God, and the power of His Christ have come, for the accuser of our brethren, who accused them before our God day and night, has been cast down."
REVELATION 12:10 NKJV

A four-year-old girl who was visiting her aunt asked
if she could have ice cream for breakfast.
Before her aunt could reply, the girl's father said,
"Sweetie, we don't eat ice cream for breakfast."
His daughter looked at him and said, "I didn't ask you."
And her aunt gave her ice cream for breakfast.

In our spiritual battles, Satan can tempt us to despair because we know that we are guilty of what he is accusing us. We look at our failures and our sins and wonder how God could possibly forgive us one more time. But if we hear a little voice telling us, "You are doomed," we can say, "I didn't ask you." We don't have to listen to anything negative about ourselves. God sees us as perfect because we are in Christ, and God only sees Him. Satan can accuse us all he wants to. God simply smiles and says, "Not guilty. The price has been paid." So any time a negative thought makes us feel bad about ourselves, we can simply say, "I didn't ask you," and ask God to cleanse us from all unrighteousness. Then we trust Him to fight our battles for us.

We know whom to ask for every good thing.

"JESUS LOVES ME"

*For I am persuaded, that neither death, nor life, nor angels,
nor principalities, nor powers, nor things present, nor things to
come, nor height, nor depth, nor any other creature, shall be able to
separate us from the love of God, which is in Christ Jesus our Lord.*
ROMANS 8:38–39 KJV

*Confusing two of his favorite songs, a three-year-old boy sang loudly,
"Jesus loves me in a one-horse open sleigh."*

There is no confusion about Jesus loving us. If there is one thing
we can fully put our trust in it is that He loves us wherever we
are and no matter what we've done. It never hurts to take a
secular song and add Jesus to it because He is the reason for all
our singing. The Bible says that "in him we live, and move, and
have our being" (Acts 17:28 KJV). Since He created us and loves
us and knows why we are here, how can we not trust Him to
lead us in the way we should go? We prove our love and trust
for Jesus in our willingness to follow Him wherever He may
take us. Nothing happens to us without His allowing it. He is
in perfect control. We can sit back and enjoy the ride when we
leave the driving to Him.

Jesus loves us everywhere, every time, every moment, every day.

Not in the Budget

My God shall supply all your need according to
His riches in glory by Christ Jesus.
PHILIPPIANS 4:19 NKJV

A four-year-old girl wanted an expensive toy for Christmas.
Her mother said, "Honey, maybe this toy is not in Santa's budget."
"Don't worry," the girl told her mother,
"Santa doesn't need money for toys."

Fortunately for us, God doesn't have a budget. He doesn't need one because He's amazingly rich! And His blessings to us are limitless. Out of His abundance He supplies everything to us. He has promised to provide for us and we trust Him to keep that promise. Sometimes we might get confused between something we truly need and something we just happen to want. But God knows the difference. He chooses for us. When we trust God, we are happy with what He gives us. God wants us to have contented lives, to be at peace, and to be joyful. Never stingy or mean, God gives us everything we require—and more! He opens His hands and pours out blessings on us daily. He says, "Try Me now in this. . .if I will not open for you the windows of heaven and pour out for you such blessing that there will not be room enough to receive it" (Malachi 3:10 NKJV). What a wonderful God!

With God, our hands are never empty of blessings.

OPEN ALL THE WAY UP

Open my eyes, that I may behold wondrous things out of Your law.
PSALM 119:18 AMP

"I like my sunglasses," a four-year-old girl told her aunt.
"They let me open my eyes all the way up."

God is like our spiritual sunglasses. He lets us open our spiritual "eyes all the way up." And when we do, what wondrous things we behold. God's law is perfect. We can trust that living right—by doing all the things He tells us to do—is for our own benefit. The reason God doesn't want us to sin is because He can see what the consequences of our wrong actions will do to us and to those around us. So we can put on our spiritual "shades," look into His commands with eyes wide open, and see all the benefits awaiting us. Following God's law gives us the choice not to sin but to live the joyful life that comes by doing right. Jesus showed us what such a life could be like. Like Him, we, too, are to be filled with compassion, love, patience, kindness, goodness, and gentleness. Now that's a wondrously abundant life! Let's behold the wonder by putting our confidence in Christ! For the more we trust Him, the more we will be like Him.

God wants us to see with our spiritual eyes
all the wonders that He has given us in His word.

Wishing Doesn't Make It So

Trust in the Lord and do good.
PSALM 37:3 NIrV

While a mother was getting ready for bed, she asked
her nine-year-old son if he wanted his regular hug and kiss,
but he was busy and said not right then.
After the mother had laid down,
the son called to her and said, "I want my hug and kiss now."
"Come in here," the mother said.
"No, you come in here," the son replied.
"I'm lying down," the mother said. "You come in here."
"I'm asleep," the boy replied, "you come in here."
"If you're asleep," said the mother, "then how are you talking to me?"
"I have my eyes closed," he replied.

God is never lying down on the job. No matter what the time of day—or night—He is ready, willing, and able to give us what we need. We don't have to wish for things because we have God's promise that He will provide. And we appreciate His gifts all the more, knowing that we don't deserve them. There's absolutely nothing we can do to earn them. Every morning we have the opportunity to live another day close to the Lord. We can go through our schedules peacefully and joyfully, trusting God to take care of whatever challenges or upsets might come our way, knowing that no matter what, good will come of it. Whenever we need loving, we can always go to God for our "hug and kiss." He adores us, His children, with an unsurpassed love.

Whether we are awake or asleep, God is taking care of us.

Secrets

A woman was telling her sister something funny that her six-year-old daughter had done. "Mommy," said the six-year-old, "don't tell my stuff."
"Okay," the mother replied.
But when the daughter went into the other room, the mother again began telling her sister what the daughter had done.
"Ah. Ah. Ah," came the little voice from the other room.
"You said you wouldn't tell."

There is no one more trustworthy than God. We can safely entrust all our secrets to Him—He knows them anyway. But God will never tell our secrets to others. When David's son Absalom rebelled and tried to take the kingdom away from his father, one of David's most trusted advisers, Ahithophel, deserted David and offered his services to Absalom. How betrayed David must have felt. Not only had his friend left him, but he was now telling all of David's secrets to Absalom. God intervened on David's behalf and caused Absalom not to believe the advice of Ahithophel. Unable to bear what he had done, Ahithophel hanged himself. (See 2 Samuel 17). Maybe we've been betrayed by a friend. But none of us has ever gone through what Jesus did when He was betrayed by Judas. Yet, when Judas led the soldiers into the Garden of Gethsemane to arrest Jesus, Jesus still called him friend (see Matthew 26:50). We may betray God but He will never betray us.

When we have a secret to keep, God is the best one to tell it to.